THE FREEDOMS OF
SUBURBIA

PAUL BARKER

F

FRANCES LINCOLN LIMITED

PUBLISHERS

FOR SALLY

The Freedoms of Suburbia
Frances Lincoln Limited
4 Torriano Mews
Torriano Avenue
London NW5 2RZ
www.franceslincoln.com

Copyright © Paul Barker 2009
Illustrations copyright, see page 240
First Frances Lincoln edition: 2009

ISBN: 978-0-7112-2978-5

Printed and bound in China

2 4 6 8 9 7 5 3 1

THE FREEDOMS OF SUBURBIA

All buildings are predictions. All predictions are wrong.
Stewart Brand, *How Buildings Learn: What Happens After They're Built* (1994)

Modernism's failure lay in its obsession with starting with a clean
slate and in its confusion of aesthetics with functional design.
The old had to be swept away and the new had, above all, to look
different. Complex blocks, flat roofs and white walls were preferred,
and semi-detached houses with pitched roofs condemned.
Giles Worsley, 'Suburban Semis for the 21st Century' (2000)

Among a million Russian cottages you'll never find even two that
are identical. Everything that lives is unique. It is unimaginable
that two people, or two wild roses, should be exactly the same.
Vasily Grossman, *Life and Fate* (1960)

The Englishman sees the whole of life embodied in his house.
Hermann Muthesius, *The English House* (1904)

Private pavements adjoining the public pavement shall be landscaped
with cobbles, or soft-landscaped with gravel or planting in soil pockets,
or a combination of these. Private pathways visible from the street shall
be of gravel or stone. All planting shall be agreed with the architect.
Leon Krier, *Poundbury Masterplan* (1988–91)

They share a dream of the house they will finally own together. One
very different from these south London flats. Their dream house,
which sounds like something from one of Simon's fantasy tales, is
in fact a farmhouse on the outskirts of Tallinn in Estonia. . . . They
speak of Estonia basically as a very, very outer London suburb.
Daniel Miller, *The Comfort of Things* (2008)

CONTENTS

*Title page and overleaf:
Ilkley, west Yorkshire.*

IN THE BEGINNING

Everything starts personally. So let me put a few biographical cards on the table. I grew up in Hebden Bridge, which was then a large Pennine textile village, or arguably a small town, surrounded by moorland. It was very close-knit, even inbred, and for decades it had had a declining population. The mills closed, and Hebden Bridge became, largely, a commuter dormitory for people who work in Manchester, Leeds or Huddersfield. It is now also very arty (my novelist friend Angela Carter called it 'the Greenwich Village of the north') and a prolific source of letters to the *Guardian*. I no longer have to explain to outsiders where it is.

Back then, I had no experience of what suburbia meant. When I eventually came to London, the places I lived in – Chelsea, Marylebone, Stepney and Kentish Town – had all been built as suburbs: the kind from which the first residents walked to work, caught the horse-bus or horse-tram, or took one of the early steam-driven Underground trains. But these places were not what most people, including me, thought of as suburbia. According the usual, unhistorical definition, this means houses built since about 1900, or possibly 1890.

About suburbs, I shared the usual prejudices. When we looked to buy our first family house, in Kentish Town in inner north London, I was determined it would be in the flat-fronted, Georgian style: the kind that Modernists approved of. The house we got was, in fact, late Victorian, but the local builder was obviously behind the times. He had used an old flat-front pattern book: there was a stucco pediment and no fanciful bay windows. The street was only a notch or two above a slum (if that). My first step in gentrification was to root up the privet in the tiny patch of front garden and to chip the enamelled name, 'Bowerhayes' off the glass panel above the door. Inside, we took off all the picture rails, bricked up any remaining fireplaces and painted the walls of all the rooms white. I sketched out a fairly uncomfortable built-in living room sofa for our carpenter to cut out of blockboard, in a design based on my admiration for the ultra-angular Rietveld chair. Now the house could take its place as truly urban, even semi-Modernist. This kind of process is faithfully recorded in Michael Frayn's comic novel, *Towards the End of the Morning*.

Much, much later I began to see the merits of all varieties of suburbia. It was *terra incognita* for me, almost like a nineteenth-century expedition into

Opposite: Folkestone suburb, Kent. The magic of crazy paving.

Africa. Here weren't dragons, or elephants, but sunrise garden gates and privet, privet, privet. My change of mind was driven partly by the absolute disasters of almost all Modernist forays into designing mass housing. We had lived in Stepney while perfectly good small terrace houses were demolished all around us in favour of monster blocks. All that was wrong with most of these houses was that they had too many people in them, and those people were too poor. It was nothing structural: architecture was neither the ailment nor the cure. My growing conviction about the merits of suburbia was strengthened by the American sociologist H.J. Gans's path-breaking and affectionate study of the most derided suburban housing designs in the United States, the cookie-cutter Levittowns.

The present essay is the eventual outcome. The framework is a personal journey through suburbia in its various shapes and sizes, from Metroland to Milton Keynes, from Letchworth to the Lakeside mall. I try to capture the way most people live now, and why they like it. I cherish suburbia's vigour and unexpectedness: a white witch in south London, artificial black swans on a mall's artificial lake, the multiple uses of crazy paving. Suburbia isn't static; it is endlessly adaptable. Its vociferous enemies fail to see that it is an essential ingredient of city life. Such critics are outnumbered many, many times by the millions for whom suburbia is a land of pleasantness, friendship and hope.

Going around with my eyes open, I have attempted to counter the usual obsessions – especially among writers on architecture and planning – with city centres and with the way of life, and opinions, of a tiny urban elite. Interwoven with my journey is other evidence, from past polemics and present plans, from literature, anthropology and sociology. All these build up to my argument, in the last two chapters, in which I cast doubt on the wisdom of too much planning. There is no harm in allowing things just to happen. The pleasures of sheer chance should not be undercut. This is how most of our towns were created.

In their traditional sponge and balsa-wood models of new developments, and then in the later computer-generated versions, British architects have always showed the future inhabitants enjoying café life, under little sunshades, with a cheery glass of red wine. It would be like holiday-time Urbino. For years, one of the few places in England where you could see something like this was inside the MetroCentre shopping mall at Gateshead. At Romano's, on the mall's upper floor, the sunshades were there, the round tables and the wine. It was a good place for a gossip. Look up, and you saw the fierce down-lights from the mall roof. The sun didn't shine on Romano's, but it didn't rain, either.

All that then changed, in much of southern England at least. Suddenly, you could hardly move for pavement tables. This was due to two unplanned changes: the weather got warmer, and anti-smoking laws meant that smokers had to sit outside. Non-Plan can be just as good as Plan, or better.

Writing passionately about downtown New York, in her great anti-planning book *The Death and Life of Great American Cities* (1961), Jane Jacobs aimed to rescue the inhabitants of the 'outdated' inner cities from contemporary derision and force-fed urban 'improvements.' It may seem paradoxical, but I feel I am paying a twenty-first-century homage to her in seeking now to rescue suburbia and suburbanites – which means most of the population – from comparably wrong-headed condescension and hostility. Mine is an argument for modesty, humility and a non-showy kind of optimism. It is, above all, an argument in defence of the freedoms of suburbia. In his *Maxims for Revolutionists*, Shaw wrote: 'Do not do unto others as you wish they should do unto you, their tastes may not be the same.'

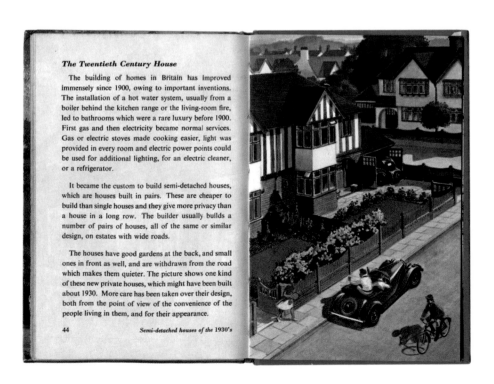

The way it was. From The Story of Houses and Homes, by Richard Bowood, illustrated by Robert Ayton. Respectful of 1930s semis, this Ladybird children's book (1963) also praises reinforced concrete flats: 'as beautiful in their way as were the best homes of the past'.

1. LIVING IN THE PRESENT

I stood, one Sunday, at the back of a special Thanksgiving service at the Baptist church on the corner of Hackney Downs. The service ended at 11.30am, so that the participants could go out to 'celebrate the end of one era and the start of a new':

> O God of burning, cleansing flame,
>> Send the fire.
> Your blood-brought gift today we claim.
>> Send the fire today!

The rivals. Opposite: An interwar semi in Mayfield Avenue, Kenton, north London. Below: A tower block is blown up in Hackney, east London.

Outside, a white banner at the top of the estate's nearest high-rise said that all twenty-two storeys would be blown up at noon. Hackney Borough Council had laid on a party: bouncy castle, halal rice and curry, doughnuts, a jazz band. An actor from *EastEnders* gave a little speech. Seventy-seven pounds of explosive detonated in three quick bangs. The block subsided like a burst balloon. A brown cloud of dust rolled across the sky. Debris settled three storeys high. One doctrinaire dream of how people were told they ought to live – but didn't want to – had vanished, like magic.

Once the piles of concrete and metal were shifted, from this and the other blocks on the estate, workmen started to build a new little suburb: two- or three-storey houses. They were a close replica of the Victorian neighbourhood the tall blocks had displaced. Those high-rise blocks were once The Future. They turned out to be a passing fashion or, rather, a transient dogma. Suburbia had won.

Almost all architectural and planning commentaries, in the press or in government publications, still speak of the suburb as an evil that must somehow be cast out. To call anything or anyone 'suburban' is to utter a put-down, an anathema, a curse.

Newly completed bay-window terrace housing in Clapton, Hackney, 1880s. Such modest homes were often demolished in favour of grandiose schemes of comprehensive redevelopment.

Yet suburbs are almost unbelievably popular. They do not merely survive: they flourish, in the teeth of all criticism, like a *leylandii* cypress or a red-flowering horse chestnut. The 'new era', which so delighted the Baptists of Hackney in north-east London, was in fact the return of the old. Suburbia resumed its grip on hearts and minds.

The demolition job in Hackney followed a trend that began in the United States in 1972, when the Pruitt-Igoe high-rise homes in St Louis were blown up. This cluster of public housing had been built, to much acclaim within the architectural profession, in 1955. Pruitt-Igoe was created by the same Japanese-American architect, Minoru Yamasaki, who went on to design the World Trade Center in New York, destroyed by terrorism in 2001. The trouble with Pruitt-Igoe was: no one wanted to live there. Children and teenagers, especially, disliked the place, and helped make it hellish for everyone else.

It always seems to take about thirty years for new ideas to cross the Atlantic. In the 1970s, south London councils were still demolishing rows of little Victorian houses in favour of megalithic concrete projects. In his 2000–8 mayoralty of London Ken Livingstone, himself a former south London borough councillor, was advised on planning by the architect Richard Rogers, chairman of the of government-commissioned 1999 Urban Task Force report. Both favoured megaliths. For a while, the dead dragon apparently rose from its grave. The alleged glamour of high-rise housing blocks was trumpeted once again. The 2008 bursting of the construction industry bubble put the dragon back in its coffin, temporarily at least. It seems that every lesson has to be re-learnt in every generation. It is sometimes said that the only lesson of history is that we do not learn from history. But we ought, perhaps, to try.

In the opening of his great work of social history, *The Making of the English Working Class*, E.P. Thompson wrote: 'I am seeking to rescue the poor stockinger, the Luddite cropper, the "obsolete" handloom weaver, the "utopian" artisan, and even the deluded follower of Joanna Southcott, from the enormous condescension of posterity.' I am perhaps taking on almost as mammoth a task. The suburbs and those who happily live in them have long been written off by all right-thinking people as beyond the pale, below the salt, and altogether past praying for. But unlike Thompson's Southcottian sectarians, the much-mocked suburbanites are, in Britain, the vast majority of the population. And it is their contemporaries who patronise and condescend to them, not posterity.

Kenton is a vivid example of the kind of place I want to celebrate. Built mainly in the 1920s and 1930s, this is a suburb that few people, other than those who live there, have ever heard of. It lies, like a gentle enigma, at the meeting point of the north-west London boroughs of Harrow and Brent. My exploration won't just be in London; nor will other countries' experience be ignored. But London and its outliers are the obvious leading case. In the late twentieth and early twenty-first centuries, the capital was booming in a similar way to that which created the swathes of interwar suburban semis, of which Kenton is one. It is worth noting that this metropolitan boom was widely unpredicted (as was the 2008 bubble-burst which followed). Up to the mid-1980s, all the experts said that London was in permanent decline, and all public policies were based on this thought. Unlike a gift horse, always look a forecast in the mouth.

Today, it is estimated, 84 per cent of people in Britain live in a form of suburbia – often in that classic creation, the semi-detached house, which is where most of the inhabitants of Kenton live. Suburbia seems to give most

*Kenton: one of the 496
'Mayfields' in Great Britain.*

people what they want most of the time, at a price they can afford. The precise design of a house is perceived as less important than other local benefits: good neighbours, good schools, good doctors, good roads, good public transport. Nor, as the urban historian F.M.L. Thompson wrote, in *The Rise of Suburbia*, can you ever understand this entire phenomenon without understanding the love of gardens. Many British environmentalists suffer acutely from the national disease of social bossiness: find out what all those people are doing, and tell them to stop it. Suburbs are often accused of being non-green. But they are very green indeed in a very obvious sense. I have sometimes thought I should start a Privet Preservation Society.

Let me focus for a moment, within Kenton, on the small but evocative world of Mayfield Avenue, which dates from 1926. There are as many varieties of suburbia as of garden-centre dahlias or hellebores, but this is the interwar variety, which newspaper picture editors always dig out of the files to illustrate some new scathing attack on suburbs by the in-house architecture critic.

The London *A–Z*, I see, lists thirty-two Mayfields, slightly tweaked to suit an estate agent's imagination. There are Mayfield Crescents, Closes, Drives, Gardens, Roads and Avenues. (There are no 'streets' in suburbia.) Suburban land developers have always liked vaguely rural names, with undertones of Housman, Elgar and Morris dancing. 'Mayfield' is popular everywhere, from Halifax to Huntingdon, from Edinburgh to Eastbourne. In England, Wales and Scotland, the streetmap.co.uk website gives a total of 496 Mayfields.

Kenton's Mayfield Avenue is lined with semis. On some of them, the original black and white gables are still intact. As elsewhere in suburbia, the houses were put together by the builders from a kit of parts whose inglenooks, deep roofs, pebbledash and fancy gabling pay distant homage to the houses that the Arts & Crafts architects, C.F.A. Voysey and M.H. Baillie Scott, built around the end of the nineteenth century. (Many twenty-first-century suburban houses, on the present outskirts of towns and villages, still echo Voysey and Baillie Scott, though ever more faintly.) More important is the fact that the avenue is handy for the Bakerloo Underground station, which fostered Kenton's suburban growth.

Like many such places, Kenton's location is hard to pin down historically. The main road is lined with shopping parades, now undercut by the store that Sainsbury's built on an old railway coalyard. The south side used to be in

Wembley, administratively (now bundled into the London Borough of Brent). The north side was, and is, in Harrow.

For many years the offices of *Gramophone* magazine were on Kenton Road. This was the bible for every aspiring Kenton householder who invested in a veneered cabinet in order to play 78 rpm shellac records of Brahms or Al Bowlly. In his social history *Austerity Britain*, published in 2008, David Kynaston reported that when, in 1948, BBC radio launched its pioneering (and comforting) daily teatime soap opera, *Mrs Dale's Diary* – which ran for twenty-one years – Dr Jim Dale and his family were aptly located in Kenton. The BBC later veiled the exact district by re-naming it 'Parkwood Hill.'

In the early twenty-first century, Mayfield Avenue's spec-development semis are around the bottom of their fashionability cycle. There is nothing smart about them. But they are amazingly adaptable containers, I'd argue, as is Kenton itself. That is one test of the Good House or the Good Neighbourhood they pass with flying colours. You can pour into these houses what you want.

They were built for the first generation to have vacuum cleaners and valve radios. The importance of owning, rather than renting, a house was beginning to exert its grip on British society, thanks to cheap land, high aspirations and the cut-price mortgages offered by the newly flourishing building societies. Previously almost everyone, of whatever social class, rented. In his 1939 novel *Coming Up for Air*, George Orwell said how much he hated the building societies for helping to destroy the open fields of Middlesex and Surrey. He described this as 'probably the cleverest racket of modern times. . . . The beauty of the building-society swindle is that your victims think you're doing them a kindness. You wallop them and they lick your hand.' Largely thanks to the interwar building boom, about a third of the houses in Britain are semi-detached: the great national balancing act between privacy and price. This is one argument Orwell lost. He was almost always sympathetic to the working class; but seldom to the aspirant lower middle class.

Take No. 40 Mayfield Avenue as a model example. The grass in the front garden was neatly mown, I noted. There was a flowering cherry and a privet hedge. The pebbledash was painted white. The gable had lost its black stripes, but the door had its original stained glass. In the driveway stood an M-reg. Honda Civic. At a glance Mayfield Avenue looked as if it had been stamped out with a template (in this resembling a Georgian terrace of the 1700s, a Barratt estate of the 1980s or a cluster of 1990s executive homes). But, as I walked along, I saw that over the past eighty years this uniformity had become less and less true.

It is important in suburbia to mark off your territory as your own. No. 40 was the only house that still used pavement-edge privet for this purpose; euonymus was now more usual. The alternatives included a brick wall (sometimes covered with variegated ivy) or wrought-iron fencing. Even the house numbers told a story, differentiating owner from owner. The most casual tactic was to stick on those slanting grey rhomboid numerals from DIY shops. Other owners went to town, like arithmeticians on a spree. No. 8 had two sets of numerals. One set, in brass, was screwed onto the door itself. The other set was on a cast iron plaque, decorated with little flowers, and fixed to the wall above three miniature *leylandii*.

I'd describe the door here as a kind of neo-gothic. Other doors had become neo-Georgian. In Mayfield Avenue, the statement your door made mattered.

Looking along Mayfield Avenue. A good ordinary street. No-parking lines hasten the move of cars into front gardens.

So did the statement made by the front garden space. Until recently, No. 10 was alone in retaining the classic design, probably unchanged since 1926 – a square of grass with a single standard rose in the dead centre – but a dry summer killed the rose. Crazy paving proliferated everywhere. No two layouts were the same. It might be all one plain colour or a liquorice-allsorts mix of pink, white, blue and grey. This was highly functional: for parking on.

Created by an Underground link, Mayfield Avenue is a paradise for cars. Even in the early days, each house was originally built with double wooden doors alongside. Behind these the owners could keep their Bullnose Morris or Austin Seven, for weekend use only. Now proper garages have been constructed in a dozen baroque styles. But most of the time, this is where the household junk is stored. Two or even three cars sit outside many houses.

Vehicles are now central to the roadside look of Mayfield Avenue, as in almost all other parts of Britain. I have kept a friendly eye on this avenue for about fifteen years. Gradually, more and more front gardens have given way to parking space, for ever-larger and more numerous cars (4 × 4s, Audis, Mercs). These are squeezed in on the crazy paving alongside Harrow council's blue, green and brown trio of colour-coded wheelie bins (ecological but very unlovely). Regret the changes or not, all this is a present-day fact of visual and social life. But none of it is irreversible. As in the past, the semi retains its readiness to adapt to future change.

The semi gives you neighbours, but not too many of them. As a social and design invention it is an extraordinary success story. Messrs Berry Brothers in St James's, off Piccadilly, sell a wine they call 'Good Ordinary Claret'. Mayfield Avenue is a Good Ordinary Street.

The avenue runs straight out into Kenton Road. Once upon a time, after the husband had gone off to the station on his way to work, the wife went out to the shopping parades with her Silver Cross pram. She compared her children's growth with fellow-shoppers over a polite cup of tea and a buttered scone. All that has gone. In Kenton, as elsewhere, shopping is done in the evenings and at the weekend.

Thinking of Dr and Mrs Dale's Kenton and 'Parkwood Hill,' the Queen Mother reportedly once said: 'It is the only way of knowing what goes on in a middle class family.' Half a century later, the families have undergone one significant change. It is Asian retailers and their customers who have kept Kenton's shopping parade from total collapse. In the nearby streets, including Mayfield Avenue, an increasing proportion of the houses now belong to Asian families, many of whom (or their parents) were thrown out of East and Central Africa by the new post-independence regimes. Here, too, Mayfield Avenue showed its adaptability. In external design, the stained glass of some doors included an Indian motif. One window was draped temporarily with a multicoloured shawl in lieu of curtains. On the crazy paving at No. 18 stood the red van of Pradip's 'Indian Sweets and Savouries'. The Kenton Road shopping parade had a trio of Pradip frontages: sweet mart, vegetarian restaurant and caterer's. Every other service was here, from cradle (the Asian-run Creative Photographics shop for births, coming of age, and marriages) to grave (an Asian undertaker's).

London itself has been created by suburbanisation. In *London: The Unique City* – the best analysis ever written on London's growth – the Danish architect and critic Steen Eiler Rasmussen emphasised that the capital has always grown by adding suburb on to suburb: so-called 'walking suburbs', at first (where you could reach your job on foot); then railway, bus and Tube suburbs; now car and van suburbs. And since Mayfield Avenue's builders cut the first sod in 1926, everywhere in Britain, both town and country, has been suburbanised.

Few villages now contain many inhabitants who have anything to do with agriculture; they are stuffed with either second-home owners or commuters, or both. William Morris's beloved village of Kelmscott, on the boundary of Oxfordshire and Gloucestershire, is the original of the Utopian, earthly-paradise landscapes in his novel *News from Nowhere*. Visiting Kelmscott, I found that only two local farmers made their living from the land. One employed three men who lived in the village. The other employed two men who both lived elsewhere. Kelmscott once had two shops and a sub post office. All three had gone. Dairy cows still munched picturesquely in the meadows running down to the upper Thames. But everywhere within reach of a big city – Manchester, Leeds, Birmingham, Bristol, Glasgow – a village is now a geographical expression, not a statement about how people make a living.

Around the edges of today's suburbanised villages, I always look out for two new kinds of dwelling: the estate of executive homes or the mobile home park, both of them togged up with hanging baskets of flowers and little cement rabbits. At Kelmscott's own mobile home estate, I noticed, the caravans were arranged in little rows and alleys, their wheels hidden behind little brick skirts.

There were plastic windmills and gnomes in the tiny gardens. The council houses, where the caravan dwellers might once have lived, had all been sold off.

Though 'suburban' remains a standard term of abuse, the many evidences of suburbia will, in due course, be cherished by conservationists, planners and even sociologists, as is the industrial terrace housing once mocked and destroyed as slums. In the past, the polemicists' off-the-peg propaganda photograph was always of the rows upon rows of such houses in Preston, the cotton town model for Dickens's Coketown in *Hard Times*. Preston is now ringed with suburbia. The industrial terraces have been demolished as supposed public health hazards, or else are now mostly inhabited by students at the University of Central Lancashire (the former Preston Polytechnic) and by the families of migrants from the Indian sub-continent.

The self-help houses the 'experts' all too often ignore: mobile home park, Exeter, Devon.

As architecture and as a version of ecological planning, such terraces are now much admired. In Manchester's Hulme district – where they were demolished in favour of a 1960s concrete nightmare – the city has attempted to reinstate them.

Suburbia need only wait for its own accolade. The wheel of fashion will turn again. Art Deco, so recently derided, has become sacrosanct. (It was the style the glitzy Post-Modernism of the 1980s and 1990s revived.) Would you ever get permission now to raze an Odeon? I await with confidence the first Grade II listed shopping mall. Ten years? Twenty? And how long before the dying craft of fixing TV aerials to roofs evokes the same nostalgia as the thatching trade?

For the time being, the rampant anti-suburbanism continues. Tristram Hunt's recent history of British cities, *Building Jerusalem*, gave much clear-minded analysis of earlier eras. But I regret that, when it came to the contemporary city, he followed the party line of the Urban Task Force report. Hunt asserted that 'The most iniquitous consequence of suburban life was its assault on the public ethos of the city.' But isn't suburbia an intrinsic part of the modern city? Hunt went on to mourn, on the basis of numerous opinion surveys, the fact that a 'detached home with a garden on monotonous, Barratt-style housing estates is where people seem to want to live'. This is an echo of the American urban historian Lewis Mumford, who wrote, in 1961, in *The City in History*:

> [The suburban] movement from the centre carries no hope or
> promise of life at a higher level. Just as our expanding technological
> universe pushes our daily existence ever further from its human
> centre, so the expanding urban universe carries its separate
> fragments ever farther from the city, leaving the individuals more
> dissociated, lonely and helpless than he probably ever was.

This has become the cut-price accepted wisdom. Suburbia is derided by everyone – except the millions who live there, and shop happily at the nearest mall. It must be doing something right. My own quest is to pin down what this is. I want to put the argument on a more rational, less snobbish footing. Suburbia is a great triumph of non-planning. There has been no great, overarching, even dictatorial vision. Much has happened almost by accident. A city is not a computer programme. It is very hard to tweak it in the way you wish. It has a life of its own. To try to talk about cities, without talking frankly about their suburbs and their appeal, is completely bizarre.

In Britain, the recent, much-trumpeted revival of inner-city living began in London and spread, for example, to Manchester, Birmingham and Leeds. The core social group were 'dinkies': double-income no-kids couples, otherwise known as 'tins' (two incomes, no sex). In the days of huge City bonuses, the two of them worked such long or erratic hours that they need somewhere near at hand, in Bethnal Green or Battersea, where they could collapse at night, preferably with a decent restaurant round the corner. The sociologist R.E. Pahl called them 'income-rich but time-poor'. The inner-city regeneration of some regional cities was a paler version of the London phenomenon: a tiny patch of 'downtown' within ten minutes of a new-minted 'gay village' (Manchester's Canal Street) or a revamped workshop district (Birmingham's Jewellery Quarter). In contrast, market researchers find that 80 per cent of the population say they would like to live in the country, with uninterrupted views all round. No dice. The suburb is, for many, the nearest substitute. It is a kind of country, at least. (The inner-city income-rich achieve a similar outcome by escaping to their second home at the weekends.) Many of the flats in supposedly glamorous high-rise towers in both Manchester and Leeds remained empty after their 2008 completion. The flats had been bought, off plan, as pure speculation, in order to be let. Beyond a certain point, you can't make, or tempt, people change their life-preferences if they don't want to. Plan or no plan.

I was in a meeting once, which was drawing up the shortlist for some housing design awards. A senior planner told us emphatically that the only way forward was to build houses to a high density on so-called 'brownfield' sites, with people tucked into the proper minimum of rooms. The current dogma, in fact. It then emerged that he himself lived in a four- or five-bedroom house in the country and, being divorced, lived there on his own. 'I need this space,' he said, in response to mildly raised eyebrows.

And this is the way it all too often is. Notoriously, architects and planners very seldom live in the sort of houses they design or argue for, especially if the houses in question are social housing. We ought by now to have learned that the worst urban disasters occur when we try to force other people to live in ways they don't want to. And, often, in ways we wouldn't want to live ourselves.

Ruralists and urbanists dominate many of the present arguments. But the town-country of suburbia is where many of the most vigorous urban innovations start: the multiplex cinema (the first of which, in Britain, opened in Milton Keynes, that city of suburbs) and the shopping mall. Built on wasteland at the edge of Gateshead in the 1980s, the MetroCentre was first full-blown mall in Britain. The American term for such growth is Edge City. Offices, warehouses and homes start to spring up around the malls. A new version of suburbia.

Most people who condemn malls seem (or pretend) never to have been to one. Malls are closely bound up with the gender politics of car ownership and working mothers. If you want to juggle your job (often part-time), your children (including the school run) and your shopping, it's very hard to do it without the second car and the one-stop shop, like MetroCentre Gateshead, Trafford Centre Manchester, Cribbs Causeway Bristol and the rest. Or, failing a full-blown mall, a vast retail park, like Fosse Park, outside Leicester.

The shock of the old: 1990s houses echo 1930s designs, though semis give way to close-knit 'executive homes' with double garages. Nantwich, Cheshire.

Malls have turned cities inside out, like an old glove. They have become new nodes of growth. Take Lakeside Thurrock, for example, built from 1987 onwards on the eastern edge of London. Around the mall have sprung up the big sheds of a retail park (Costco, IKEA), many warehouses and offices – and a 600-acre 'new community' called Chafford Hundred. Empty chalk quarries have become the Gorges Nature Park. Many of the Chafford Hundred house designs evoke interwar suburbia. There is Wimpey's 'Tudor' style (diluted Baillie Scott). Or there is a Barratt design, which lines up houses with garages and steeply pitched roofs (Voysey for the twenty-first century). Hands are wrung, regulations drafted, editorials written, but the trend goes on.

Edge City, which is Non-Plan in action, is only the most extreme example of what is happening. Almost everywhere has been suburbanised, both socially and (often) in design. Suburban pride in ownership is omnipresent. Look at any former council-house estate. Front doors tell the story of the right-to-buy. The council's doors have been removed. From Newcastle to Plymouth, from Cardiff to Ipswich, the suburbanite replacements vary between Costa Brava (the heavy Spanish style, with bright varnished panels) and Barbara Cartland (neo-Regency, with glazed fanlight). Both versions are tougher than the old doors. There is no glass you can

This is precisely where 1930s semis ground to a halt after the London County Council's Green Belt Act, 1938 (reinforced by wartime shortages of materials). Pony paddocks are an exurbia trademark.

easily knock in; the woodwork is stronger. But the main point, as on Mayfield Avenue, is to say: this is my house, not anyone else's. The message is rubbed in by the carriage lamps, the new paint, and even (sometimes) a little oriel window above the front door.

In thinking about suburbia, we are talking about a new use of space, to which the old arguments about cities do not apply. Given the importance of the car in all this, we are also talking about a new psychology of time. After all, even city centres are not what they were: they are more and more like leisure parks. Nobody really intended, or planned, this. You can't nail cities down: they are as elusive as a professional escapologist.

Dikes and ditches can be built to direct the stream of urban change one way or another. But the stream carries on. A study of the way Paris and London grew, in the second half of the twentieth century, drew many distinctions between south-east England and the Ile de France. The most striking is the way Paris has flowed into its surroundings without interruption, whereas London has been surrounded by the Great Dike of the green belt. But the economic and demographic pressure of London did not diminish. It re-emerged across the green belt, in a ring of small towns and formerly independent cities. These became 'exurbs': suburbs divided from the core city by a veil of countryside or semi-countryside. The Paris version is slightly different. Though Paris has no green belt, the regional plan did have certain controls on what could be built and where. French developers, like their British counterparts, wanted to hop across the boundary of planning control. They did so. Research shows that the greatest growth of jobs and houses around Paris is now many, many miles from the old metropolitan centre.

As I left London and drove north towards Potters Bar in Hertfordshire, I saw on my left a wide empty field, of the kind agriculture now creates. I could identify where the hedgerows had been cut down. A stream wound across the field, before it disappeared into a culvert behind a muddle of old planks and plastic. Under a pylon, behind a wall, were the caravans of a gypsy mobile home park. A suburbanite potted plant adorned the entrance. Beyond the empty field was the high embankment of the M25. The traffic hissed, like waves against rocks.

The field was cut off from the lane in front of the first row of Potters Bar houses by a line of hawthorn bushes and chain-link wire fencing. Trapped behind the wire were old shopping bags, a decaying car seat and a discarded pallet. This was the green belt. Earlier, on the other side of the M25, I had seen where the rows of 1930s semis had come to an abrupt halt – sliced off as neatly as a Madeira cake – in tribute to the London County Council's Green Belt Act of 1938. Those who fought for a green belt never foresaw that one of its main consequences for London would be to allow an easy route for an orbital motorway. A US-style parkway, in fact. Thanks to the green belt, the M25 much predated any Paris equivalent.

Potters Bar is one of the small towns around London that took the displaced impact of the capital's growth. There is now a cliff-like block in the middle of town, at the corner of Mutton Lane. This is the British head office of the Canada Life assurance company. But most of the people of Potters Bar either commute south into London each day, or travel east, west or north to other exurbs or suburbs. For evenings and weekends, Potters Bar offers the usual array of nail bars and hair salons. London, which was once a hub, has become an ever more polycentric network. Besides Potters Bar, other examples of exurbs around London would include St Albans, Chelmsford, Sevenoaks and Slough; around Manchester, Altrincham and Southport; around Leeds, Skipton and Ilkley.

Suburbia and exurbia aren't always middle class. The working class versions tend to have been built by local authorities – for example, Manchester's Wythenshawe, Birmingham's The Wood, Liverpool's Speke, Glasgow's Easterhouse, Edinburgh's

Wester Hailes (a recurrent crime scene for Inspector Rebus in Ian Rankin thrillers), London's Becontree. On the whole, these versions, being built according to bureaucratic rules, rather than the rules of what people might actually want, have worked out worse.

When they were built, the postwar New Towns were intended to be self-contained. But all of them have become sub-species of suburbia or exurbia. Even entire cities have become exurbs. Halfway between Oxford and London, on the edge of High Wycombe, the motorway through the Chilterns is now lined with out-of-town stores, many of them pretending to be brick-built barns. Structurally, Oxford is to early twenty-first-century London what Hampstead was to mid-twentieth-century London. The Oxford intelligentsia catch the shuttle bus (the Oxford Tube) in and out of central London, just as their Hampstead predecessors took the Underground's Northern line. With its suburbs and exurbs, from Oxford to Southend, and from Cambridge to Brighton, London is now a 100-mile city. This is an outcome nobody planned.

Individualism blossoms. Right-to-buy council house at Silvertown, London Docklands.

2. THREE SNAPSHOTS

SUBURBIA AS DESTINY

Suburbia is a secret world. In Croydon I met my first ever witch. But my earliest impression that day was: Croydon is a city of lost people. Walking from the station, I had never been asked the way so often. Some of those asking me for guidance were looking for the Home Office's ghoulish cathedral of immigration and asylum red tape, Lunar House (a name Jonathan Swift would have been pleased to invent). Others were just muddled by the dug-up streets. I have never been to Croydon, I think, when the streets were *not* dug up. The worst moment was when they decided to create a new network of trams across the suburbs of this mega-suburb. That project ended up costing a lot of money for little benefit. It demonstrated yet again that nothing ever turns out the way planners expect. In the 1950s and 1960s – as also in Coventry, Hull and Plymouth, for example – broad highways were driven through the heart of Croydon. In Glasgow they even pushed an entire motorway through, in imitation of the megalomaniac dreams of Robert Moses, the all-powerful New York planner who is the chief target of Jane Jacobs's anti-planning onslaught. (For Glasgow as a plan-created nightmare, see *Lanark*, Alasdair Gray's astonishing dystopian fantasy, published in 1981.) Foreshadowing Canary Wharf, Croydon was to be 'a mini-Manhattan'. The breadth of those roads made it fairly easy to add tramlines, to flank the cars.

Even in the mid-morning drizzle, I could tell that Croydon was still a boom suburb. When the planners' fashion was for forcing offices to quit central London, firms simply hopped 18 minutes down the Brighton line to Croydon, which was then an independent Surrey borough. It never became Manhattan, but it was a plausible imitation of Middle America: the Docklands of its day. Office towers rose more or less at random. Suburbia is often portrayed as just being about homes, rest and recuperation. But suburbs are increasingly about work, also. More and more firms follow the 1930s example of the factories which J.B. Priestley, in his *English Journey*, observed rising along the Great West Road out of London. There's no need to commute into the central city: you now drive in a whirl of new directions which public transport can hardly help you with.

Two sides of Croydon. Opposite: Street market. Below: Offices, including a twenty-three-storey 1960s block designed by Richard Seifert & Partners.

One of Croydon's towers is the headquarters of Nestlé UK plc. England is meeker in its populism than the United States. I was sorry to see that the tower wasn't shaped like a jar of instant coffee. But, nearby, Croydon had a fine twenty-three-storey, eight-sided block, built by the office of the commercial architect Richard Seifert in its best Centre Point style. A good place for a 1960s heritage centre, I thought. As lunchtime approached, the wine bars of Croydon filled up with young women, brown and white skinned, laughing together. The real town centre was a three-tier shopping plaza, the Whitgift Centre, as busy as an old-style market arcade.

In the plaza I wandered into Jigsaw World: puzzles of Terry Pratchett's Discworld, of bosomy pin-ups, of your own digital photos, with a full supporting be-jigsawed cast of bears, dolphins, castles, country maidens, country cottages and Sealyhams. Croydon is jigsaw city. It continually re-shapes itself, and it can be hard to see how the pieces fit together. Ottima Gifts was like a jigsaw of bad taste: 'collectables with attitude'. A mug said: 'Smoking is My Choice, so Fuck Off'. A cardboard box contained Dolly: The Sexy Inflatable Sheep. Another had the Pecker Dumbbell: 'Add strength to your length.' The Bad Taste Bears were Pooh-type figurines in a selection of very non-A.A. Milne postures: puffing a cigarette, picking nose dirt, obesely boasting that 'I beat anorexia', tied up in a cellar next to a whip-waving dominatrix.

D.H. Lawrence, who taught here, would recognise almost nothing today, except the fancy nineteenth-century town hall. Queen Victoria sat solid and bronze on a plinth outside. A stone frieze proclaimed Croydon's Late Victorian aims: Health, Study, Religion, Recreation, Music. But most of this 1890s extravaganza had been gutted, to make space for the David Lean Cinema (Lean was born here), an excellent library, an art gallery, a borough museum and a pretty café in which a modest couple held hands in the corner. A remake, for the twenty-first century, of one of Lean's best-known films, *Brief Encounter*.

The museum had a drawing of one of Croydon's 1960s skyscrapers by Malcolm McLaren, manager of the Sex Pistols and Britain's founder of punk, who was at art school here. There was also a 1930s banner from the Croydon branch of the Women's International League for Peace and Freedom, founded during the First World War. Croydon likes to memorialise the role it played in freedoms of various kinds.

Edwardian mansion block, Croydon, with ground-level shops.

A little glass box contained a modest rosary: brown beads, tarnished crucifix. What was this about? An interactive screen told me that this was the rosary handed to a young man, Derek Bentley, after he was arrested in 1952, along with Christopher Craig. The two of them were trying to rob a Croydon warehouse. They were caught on the roof. Craig shot a policeman dead. Both men were found guilty of murder. Craig was the leader. The unarmed Bentley was of low IQ and fatally uttered the words, 'Let him have it.' Being under-age, Craig was sentenced to imprisonment, and eventually released. Petitions brought Bentley no reprieve. In 1953, he was hanged. You could argue that he didn't die completely in vain. His case was one of those – along with Timothy Evans, wrongly executed for a crime the serial killer John Christie had committed, and Ruth Ellis, the last woman ever to be hanged in Britain – which fuelled a public campaign to end capital punishment. It was finally abolished in Britain as one of the social reforms brought about by Harold Wilson's liberalising government of 1964–70.

Today's Croydon owes everything to the aeroplane. At the town hall, outside the library, a sale of books included the publications of the Croydon Airport Society: *Croydon and the Battle of Britain* and *Tails of the Fifties: An Anthology of Aviation Memories*. For twenty years, between the two world wars, 'London Airport' meant Croydon airport. Amy Johnson flew from here. Businesses mushroomed. There is still an Aerodrome Hotel. The airport is long gone, but its successor, Gatwick, is only just along the way. During the last months of the 1939–45 war, Hitler's first secret weapon, the V1 flying bomb – a pilotless aircraft packed with high explosive – regularly ran out of fuel short of central London, and landed on Croydon. With characteristic chutzpah, Croydon shook itself and used the empty space as more room for mid-American suburban dreams. One landmark now is the twin towers of an old power station, painted with the familiar yellow and blue strips. This is the IKEA store for south London. Your personal domestic magic, in a flat-pack.

From her base in a rather shabby Croydon semi, Seldiy Bate offered her own alternative dose of magic. I rang the doorbell and said hello. Seldiy called herself 'an ageing hippy', and laughed. She had the right gypsyish look (an oblique tribute to D.H. Lawrence?): long dark hair, velvet blouse, green skirt with lace, silver ring on her left hand. She and her husband, Nigel, had just moved into the house, so there was little furniture. But there was an Aladdin's cave of objects: a shepherd's crook, a ritual sword (I was shown it but not allowed to touch), an old ouija board, a huge Bible, the memoirs of Aleister Crowley, a computer which Seldiy sometimes used for plotting planetary positions. She had Robert Graves's *The White Goddess* always at her bedside. She showed me a ceramic bird: 'The wren is the king of the New Year.'

She was rather mysterious about her first name (which is pronounced Zeldy). It was perhaps a version of Isolde, she said, or perhaps of Griselda – legendary ladies both. From childhood she apparently lived surrounded by mysteries. Her father was a theosophist. Various relatives were pagans or, more precisely, Wiccans (witches, to the rest of the world). A cousin taught her how to read the tarot.

She made her living mostly by divination, she told me. When she and Nigel were married (or 'handfast') according to Wiccan rites, the 'king of the witches' Alex Sanders gave them two paintings, both of which were hanging on the wall. The Moon Goddess had three candles on her head; the Sun God had one candle. They could have been framed album covers for The Grateful Dead, or some other West Coast group of half a century ago. The pictures hung behind several cages of friendly rats, which belonged to Seldiy's daughter, Madeleine. They had names like Thor and Odin.

Seldiy Bate was serious about what she did, but not pretentious. 'I'm only a lousy fortune teller. There *is* a pattern to people's lives. I try to see it. But you always have free will. Nothing I say is 100 per cent certain. Otherwise, I'd be God, and I'm not God.' When Seldiy was asked to forecast the previous year's Grand National, she wouldn't do it till the morning of the race. In suburbia, even crystal-gazers are cautious. 'I didn't just want to be psychic. I wanted to know what the going was like, and read the form.' She chose four horses. Three of them, she said, came in the first four, but she herself won nothing, because she bet on all four. She bought a lottery ticket most weeks, but her best win so far was £30. 'We spent it on a curry.'

She was a musician and performance artist, as well as a soothsayer. She read palms and would sometimes gaze into a crystal. But her main divination method was to read runes. These are a Teutonic alphabet of uncertain origin. She spilled a set of tiles out on the floor for me to see. The twenty-four letters looked rather like Greek, written with your non-writing hand while looking in a mirror. In mythology, Odin discovered runes by hanging for nine nights, fasting and wounded, on the World Ash, Yggdrasil. Nearer our own time, Himmler was fascinated by runes. The angular initials on the collars of the SS uniform were a double rune.

Each runic letter has its set of meanings, like tarot cards. Seldiy said she spread them out in a rapid circle for each divination. 'They act as a trigger. I get a picture in my mind. But whatever I say, it never means you can just sit back and let the future happen. That's how Macbeth got his downfall. He thought "no child of woman born" could harm him. But he didn't read it right. If I say, "You could be a great sculptor," it means that the *potential* is definitely there. But you have to do something about it, get the skills and persevere. A sculpture doesn't make itself. You don't get owt for nowt. People are in charge of their own destiny.'

In central Croydon, destiny seemed to mean shopping. Perhaps it was always like this. One store front from a century ago was covered with terracotta offers, all intended 'For Use and Beauty' (the phrase a commercial homage to

William Morris): millinery, ribbons, lace, gloves, silks, dresses, mantles, linens. On the converted ground floor, a branch of Nando's claimed it 'put the chic in chicken'. A stall in the middle of the street advised: 'Make sure your child carries your contact details at all times' and 'Free child-safe wristbands available here'. Through a gate I saw the sixteenth-century almshouses of the Hospital of the Holy Trinity. Over the entry was the motto: *Qui Dat Pauperi Non Indigebit* ('he who gives to the poor shall not want'). At the Whitgift Centre, the eating places included: Anna's Thai, Bar Ispani, Café Venezia, Auberge, and English & Continental. In Croydon, suburbia means choices, choices, choices.

SUBURBIA AS TIME MACHINE

Bromley, next door to Croydon, is the setting for a classic comic novel of suburbia: H.G. Wells's *The History of Mr Polly*. Published in 1910, it is based on Wells's own upbringing at this south-western edge of London. One day, in Bromley, Alfred Polly saw his first ever Americans. In those neolithic days, before Hollywood invented talkies, even the sound of an American voice was a great rarity. What impressed Mr Polly about those transatlantic visitors was 'that they were always in a kind of quiet hurry, and very determined and methodical people – much more so than any English he knew'.

Everything in the United States turns up in Britain eventually. Suburbia now is a potent mixture of striving and relaxing, evocative of American self-improvement handbooks. The novelist Harif Kureishi also grew up in Bromley. In *The Buddha of Suburbia*, published ninety years after Wells's novel, Kureishi is heavily ironical about his immigrant father's struggle to better himself. There's nothing smart about suburbia: this seems to be Kureishi's message. But you can have cosiness instead. Some commentators – for example, the LSE sociologist Roger Silverstone, in his *Visions of Suburbia* – have seen Bromley as the archetypal suburb. In its self-evident prosperity, it may well be what many other suburbs aspire to.

Bromley still describes itself in postal addresses as 'Kent', even though it is administratively an outer borough of London. The estate agents by the railway station were more realistic. Their shop-window poster said 'Completely London, Completely Bromley'. On the opposite side of the street was the vast red-brick pile of the Royal Bank of Scotland insurance division's offices.

J.D. Wetherspoon's had renamed the adjacent pub, also red-brick, The Richmal Crompton. Apparently the author of the Just William series used to teach classics at Bromley High School. The tranquil streets must have been disrupted daily by William Brown and Ginger, pursued by a tearful Violet Elizabeth Bott.

H.G. Wells was not completely forgotten. I walked up the high street, past Bang & Olufsen, Laura Ashley and the Premier Houseware shop, selling 'Welcome' mats, mops and bamboo garden-canes. In homage, I looked up at the blue plaque that marked Wells's birthplace. It was fixed on to what remains of a Victorian façade, between Primark and Mothercare. His father's china shop had long since gone. The high street was full of people scurrying along the pedestrianised zone, between stallholders crying out their cheap tangerines, their award-winning sausages and their special Kentish cobnuts. Quite reasonably, Mr Polly might guess that the high street now was full of Americans, forever making haste.

Given his lifelong hobby of seduction, Wells would have been pleased that the shop facing his plaque was an Ann Summers sex store. The window displays have toned down in recent years: no crotchless knickers or nipple-display bras. Instead, an all-white show of underwear, with the come-on 'Buy a bra and get a free thong' Young women giggled as they went past the shop, and only women went into it. Central Bromley was a retail heaven: nothing but shops, from the little stall run by The Will Writing Service to a huge mall,

Below: Richmal Crompton taught in Bromley until her books took off. William did his bit in 1941. Bottom: Advertisement from The Ideal Home magazine, 1936.

Time will tell you how wise you were to choose your home on one of

MORRELL'S

ESTATES at : BROMLEY, WEST WICKHAM, HAYES, PETT'S WOOD, ORPINGTON & CHELSFIELD, KENT   also ELTHAM, S.E.9, and HERNE HILL, S.E.24.

Illustrated on the left is MORRELL'S A14WS Type. Spacious and luxuriously fitted Lounge, Dining Room, Kitchen, 4 Bedrooms, Bathroom, etc.   Large Garage provided.

£1,350 Freehold 31/7 Weekly

Write for illustrated Brochure of 61 different types of Houses, Bungalows, Flats and Maisonettes to : MORRELL (BUILDERS), LTD., Desk ID. '' Terminal House,'' 52, Grosvenor Gardens, S.W. 'Phone : Sloane 7176.

A rabbit denotes Level 2 parking at The Glades mall, Bromley. Other levels are represented by a butterfly and a squirrel.

The Glades, slotted into the middle of town, inside a busy ring road. In downtown Bromley – as with Croydon and D.H. Lawrence – hardly a single building remained that Wells saw when he grew up here.

If 'suburb' implies stability, even stasis, the word needs updating. The twentieth century was, historically, a great destroyer. Everything in central Bromley was as fluid as a wave-motion leisure pool or a domestic jacuzzi. It was in flux, not stasis. There was an obsessive pursuit of the new. Politically, this has been a vigorously Tory borough. It twice led the outer London boroughs' revolts that ejected Ken Livingstone from his London throne (first, in 1986, as the last leader of the Greater London Council and then, in 2008, as the first directly elected mayor). But, culturally, central Bromley is an assiduous wiper-out, like those 'magic' drawing sets where a child can erase a picture and start again. Hanif Kureishi writes about his father meeting a new love, Mrs Eva Kay, in The King's Head pub. Hunting for the pub, I found that it had been transmogrified into a branch of the Northern Rock building society, the discredited huckster of ultra-cheap home-purchase loans. Contrariwise, the former National Provincial bank, across the street, had become a fancy new pub, The Partridge, with grand leather sofas, cubbyholes and waitresses in embroidered waistcoats. Next door was The Walkabout pub, with its Australian bar. Whichever dream you want, sir (or madam) . . . Some of the dreams were unexpected. One of Kureishi's teenage near-neighbours grew up to be Siouxsie Sioux, the punk-rock singer. Like McLaren in Croydon, she walked the musical road first trodden by the American pioneers of punk, the New York Dolls.

In *The Time Machine*, H.G. Wells's time traveller found that in AD 802701 life on earth was divided between the Underground World, inhabited by the brutal, ugly Morlocks, and the Upper World, inhabited by the Eloi. The Eloi, he noted, had 'a Dresden china type of prettiness'. Unlike the Morlock proletariat, they lived a soft life, in houses decorated with stained glass. A suburban vision, you might say.

As always, Wells's 1895 future-gazing tended to get a lot of things right. Here in Bromley – a land fit for the Eloi? – it seemed to me that the past *was* the future. The Marks & Spencer store, which fronted on to both The Glades mall and the high street, had a display of retro living: a reverie of mansions such as Uppark in Sussex, in its imperial heyday, where Wells's mother was housekeeper. For your kitchen, a butcher's block, a stockpot and an egg poacher; for your dining room, the 'Malabar' collection, 'crafted predominantly from mango wood'; for your lounge, a 'Spencer' sofa, a 'Lichfield' occasional table and 'Regal damask' curtains. As it happens, Uppark itself is now almost entirely repro, having been expensively restored by the National Trust after a disastrous fire.

The future is also the past. 'The past is never dead,' William Faulkner said. 'It's not even the past.' This sounds like an epigraph to *On the Origin of Species*. Charles Darwin was another Bromley man, by adoption if not by birth. The borough includes Darwin's house on the Downs, where he completed his masterwork: unarguably the most influential book published in the entire nineteenth century. And near the house is Biggin Hill airfield, from where Spitfires helped to see off the Luftwaffe planes that hoped to bring to Britain the benefits of Nazi Germany's bastardized Darwinism. Siouxsie Sioux said that one of the things she hated about suburbia was 'old people . . . always going on about Hitler' (as witness that Croydon display of local history books).

In places that I don't know, I often wander into either the magistrates' court (where these days I am usually the only, much stared-at public visitor) or the local library. Both, in their different ways, give you an acute feel for how the place ticks. Suburbs are about families and children. In Bromley, I only had to go into the borough library to see why anyone might think that this was a good place to bring up a child. It was clean, calm and well stocked with books. It is sad that Labour local councils are usually Scrooges with their library budgets, Tory boroughs lavish. It should be the other way round. Books are one road to freedom.

A griffin of reconstituted stone on the gate pier of a mock-Tudor house, Bromley.

Away from the high street and the mall, the roads of Bromley are lined with the red roofs and stucco of interwar semi-detached suburbia. Along these roads, boys and girls came out of school in their uniforms, just as William Brown once did. They walked past the *leylandii*, the berberis and the occasional spotted laurel. Those who were not on their mobiles to friends or family argued about where to find the cheapest pizza.

The Bromley Waitrose, with its vast parking lot, traded on its unique selling proposition. It was a People Like Us store. If you regularly went here (or to any other Waitrose), it was not really for the food or the drink, but in order to shop PLU-style. No riffraff hunting for cut-price offers. The store offered its shoppers a warm, prosperous, look-at-us feeling. But I had walked down in the direction of the store behind a short, bearded, elderly man in flat cap, hound's-tooth tweed jacket, beige stay-pressed trousers and polished pale-brown shoes. He reminded me of men going out for bowls competition days, years ago, in Yorkshire. He ignored a 'Fish & Chips £3.10' offer, which would 'include bread, butter and a cup of tea', and went down into an urban hollow between Waitrose's huge air-conditioning extractor units and the bright new neo-Victorian police station. I saw here an ugly brick building, which looked as if it had been stranded by history. It called itself the H.G. Wells Centre. A red-faced man and his anxious-looking wife were coming out of the side door. It was the headquarters of the Bromley Labour Party, optimistically displaying a placard of New Labour's red rose.

I felt like a suburban time traveller. With the Eloi-land of Waitrose and The Glades behind me, I had stumbled into a subterranean Morlock world. The man with the flat cap went inside. Behind a protective railing, a cramped outer terrace was full of men and two women, drinking the afternoon away. A notice offered cut-price beer. In Wells's vision, the Morlocks finally won. But not here. Most afternoon drinkers had opted for the charms of The Richmal Crompton. When I rang, Bromley council confirmed to me that it had four Labour members, against seven Liberal Democrats and forty-nine Tories. There aren't many Labour voters in any city's outer suburbs.

SUBURBIA AS CITY EDGE

Basildon and Dagenham are a pair of unheavenly twins. Basildon is on the Essex side of the M25. Dagenham is a few miles away, on the London side. Both are examples of top-down planning. Both were given an unexpected bright new centre, when the Lakeside mall was parachuted down in between them. Dagenham is dominated by the London County Council's gargantuan interwar Becontree housing estate. Basildon was built by the state as one of the first postwar New Towns. Unplanned, a glitzy commercial mall gave them a breath of life, and extra dose of freedom. It is Edge City at full throttle.

Basildon was invented after the Second World War by Clement Attlee's Labour government in order to give east Londoners a better life. Even now, if you go out to Basildon through older-established east London you see what the people of the New Town left behind. Much of East and West Ham – united as the borough of Newham – is poverty-stricken. Not all is gloom: the shops and market on Green Street, Upton Park, just along from the West Ham soccer stadium, are among the liveliest multiracial experiences in the capital. But Newham is regularly listed as one of the three most deprived areas in England. Today many hopes rest on a beneficent aftermath of the 2012 Olympics, and on the jobs generated by Stratford City, the planned new shopping mall and office centre, tucked into the armpit of the Olympics site. But back in the 1940s, the bombed boroughs had other ideas. They petitioned for the establishment of Basildon, with its winding roads, cul-de-sacs and grass verges. The 'new East End' is Essex. It is a symbol of a kind of freedom, although not all of that dream has been delivered. When the Thames Gateway regeneration project offered compensation money to 3,500 people whose homes it was demolishing in the rundown dockside district of Canning Town, they mostly used it to go off into Essex. The lure was magnetic.

Like Wigan when George Orwell went there, Basildon and its next-door neighbour Billericay are cues for an easy laugh. Wigan meant servitude, living in jerry-built

A New Town on its uppers. Basildon town centre has many offers of 'cash loans' and 'cheque advances'.

houses and working (in between slumps) in the cotton mills. The Essex stretch of territory along the Thames estuary was always a land of liberty.

Before the New Town came, this part of Essex was known for its 'plotlands', where do-it-yourself houses sprang up along the Southend railway line. A gentle anarchist Colin Ward – a hero to all libertarians – writes lovingly about such phenomena in his book *Arcadia for All: The Legacy of a Makeshift Landscape* (1984), co-authored with Dennis Hardy. After the 1871 Bank Holidays Act, east Londoners got into the habit of cheap day excursions for a stroll along Southend or Clacton pier. Agriculture was depressed, land was cheap. Special auctions, held at railway hotels, encouraged them to buy a little weekend or holiday place: 'plots for £5'. For that price you got a frontage of 20 feet and a depth of 100 feet on a hypothetical grid of roads, pegged out among the local scrub. To begin with, the new owners did come out for the weekend, camping out. Then they built a shack, or bought an old railway carriage, and the shack or carriage became a house. (You can see such converted carriages, still, at the edge of many British seaside towns or at the fringes of woodlands.) In the end, they moved in for good, and commuted back into London for work. They created a landscape which was messy: American rather than English; New Jersey UK. The planners got their revenge. Basildon New Town was designated specifically as a way to destroy the plotlands houses. Fifty years on, the few of these houses that remain are Heritage Basildon, just as Wigan has its Heritage Pier.

Under an estuary sky I walked along the wooded Plotlands Trail, up what used to be First, Second, Third and Fourth Avenues. Coaches bring schoolchildren here on history trips. The house names were a hymn to homeliness. The descriptive: Cosy Nook, View Grand, Windy Ridge. The imperial: Everest, Canada, Mandalay. The horticultural: Willows, The Beeches, The Laurels. The bookish: Deo Juvante, Mon Ami, Protem. The uxorious: Etheldene, Irene Rose, Marzoni (ma's only). The delighted: Joyway, Joyville, Myowna, The Ark, Oasis – and Happiness.

The people of Basildon are the same sort of people who came, originally, of their own accord: displaced Cockneys, mostly. A street in the centre offered Robin's Pie & Mash: 'Service and civility our speciality'. Basildon's residents were never wholly trapped into a unified, pre-planned way of living. When the New Town corporation laid out the first streets, they allotted one garage to every six houses. They soon had to scale it up to one for two, then one for

Markets have defied all predictions, and prosper. As at Croydon, so here at Basildon.

one. Basildon is a town of big but old cars: Volvos, Mercedes, Audis, even the occasional Rolls Royce. Along every crescent and cul-de-sac, Cockneys have been at work. Plain yellow-brick houses, carefully designed to echo traditional Essex building styles, have been re-fronted: imitation-stone cladding, panelled doors, elaborate wooden porches, leaded lights, little fences, chains.

The first boy's name I heard called out across Town Square was 'Darren'. He wore high-tongued trainers, too heavy for anyone to run in. Pure fashion. This is territory Mr Pooter would recognise. Today his high-dressing son, Lupin, would no longer live in the north London suburb where *The Diary of a Nobody* was set in 1892. He would be one of the young Essex dwellers who flooded into Fenchurch Street or Stratford East station every weekday morning, to try to keep the City of London and Canary Wharf going.

Indexes of poverty were here, among signs of prosperity. Cheek by jowl with two pawnbrokers, I saw other shops touting: 'Cash lent on jewellery', 'The UK's No. 1 for cheque cashing, cheque advance and cash loans', 'Cheques cashed for 7 per cent'. A clothes shop stated: 'Many items £5 or less'. The Argos store said that its catalogue was 'The essential book of choice and value'. The centre of Basildon was mostly tacky and unkempt. A blue-painted Portakabin housed the 'Basildon town police unit'. A rather sexy bronze of a mother and child (1962) evoked the early high ideals. These great hopes have now been shunted off to a smarter square with a millennium-funded glass campanile, a pavement café and a small theatre, which advertised a Dusty Springfield tribute singer.

In spite of the planners' best efforts, Basildon has sifted itself out socially. I knocked on the door of a large corner house that had been covered with cream plaster, and brown-painted strips of wood. Inside, it was a private paradise. To the right, a pool room, where a young man was rocking a baby in its pram. The baby's mother, Julie, let me in. She lived here with her own mother, Jenny, the baby's grandmother. The paving behind the house was roofed in transparent plastic, with white cotton under it, to cut down the heat and the glare. The garden was almost wholly taken up with a pond full of koi carp, large, blotchy, red and white. The back of the house was an aviary, I was told, before it was turned over to plants and fish.

A bar curved across one corner of the garden. I saw that the bar space was full of brown cardboard boxes. 'Oh, that's Proctor & Gamble,' Jenny said. 'They're free samples. That's my evening job.' She and another daughter took them round together. 'People are funny. They won't, sometimes, even accept something free. But that's the way it is.' She said: 'We used to have a windmill over the porch, out front. It turned with the wind. Taxi drivers used it as a landmark. Everybody loved it. We bought it from an antiques shop for £80 or so. But vandals threw bricks at it. They tied a string across the road and pulled it off. Nobody wants to see anyone get on.' But she was determined to make use of her freedom to get on.

The bottom dog among Basildon's neighbourhoods is Vange. 'Have you ever been to Vange?' one local woman asked me. 'Be careful if you ever do. I'd never go to Vange on a Saturday night.' When I went there, admittedly not on a Saturday night, Vange seemed scruffy but not very threatening. At Basildon magistrates' court, the first case I watched was a man from Vange. Tattoos covered both his arms. On the elbow nearest me he had a blue and red spider's web. His case was held over because a witness couldn't, or wouldn't, come. The next young man said he was studying in Southend. He went into a shop to try on a pair of jeans, and walked out with them under his old jeans. He was fined. A third young man was fined for peddling without a licence.

Basildon's St Nicholas's church, on a low Essex hill, dates back to the fourteenth century. The graveyard looked neglected: wild and overgrown, a sea of cow parsley. It was full of Annies, Lilys, Alberts, Roses, Reginalds, Hildas, Mays, Florences, Ernests. Many of the gravestones were heart-shaped. One tilting headstone was held up by a Dexion angle truss. Mary Elizabeth Riley died at the age of eighty-eight. The verse was headed 'In loving memory of Mum':

> Duty was her watchword,
> Faith her lamp in times of strife,
> Many were the sorrows
> And the burdens of her life.
> But bravely and with dignity
> She fought each bitter test.
> Now with honour and with hope
> She goes unto her rest.

There were clean white military graves, from 47779 Private H.J.L. Larkin, 25 November 1918, onwards. A new grave was marked with 'Dad' in bright-red nylon,

The new version of a town centre. Skyline of Lakeside shopping mall, off the east London leg of the M25. Photographed from the rooftop car park.

and pink and green artificial peonies. Two young girls came to look at the grave. Their white T-shirts advertised Calvin Klein.

From the churchyard, I planned to go straight on to Dagenham, but I was tugged into the Lakeside mall as if by a magnet. Princess Alexandra came here in 1990 to declare it open. It soon became the true centre of both Basildon and Dagenham. Chafford Hundred is Lakeside's own cosy little suburb. The big difference between the houses here and those in interwar suburbs is space. Land is now much dearer, thanks partly to the invention of the green belt. But the desire for space isn't easily killed. There were terrace houses at Chafford Hundred, but they were just a transit zone. A terrace, here, always meant 'starter homes': the bottom-rung option before you moved on to an 'executive home', with its design overtones of Mayfield Avenue. A man was standing outside his Chafford Hundred house in his djellaba to have a cigarette. He looked out across the quarry pools of the Gorges Nature Park towards the dome and spire of the mall. 'It's a good place to live,' he said. 'Such good access, so near to the M25, and then there's Lakeside.' If you want to walk to the mall, there's a high pedestrian bridge linking it to Chafford Hundred railway station.

I went into Lakeside through 'Lillywhites, Piccadilly Circus', 20 miles from Piccadilly. The store had shelf after shelf of white trainers and Premium Club T-shirts, though not as many for West Ham as I expected. It is not true that all malls are alike. Lakeside has an ineradicable east London feel. At the information desk, on an earlier visit, I had bought a postcard that showed the mall lit up by night, with fireworks exploding above it. This was how the management wanted you to remember it: a fun structure in the Clacton, Margate or Blackpool tradition.

Lakeside has all the usual features of a mall. The car parks are enormous. In the mall's early days a fountain of blue water bubbled up outside, beside a fluttering display of flags. A bigger mall, built in an old chalk quarry outside Dartford, Kent, was named Bluewater after this same feature. At Lakeside the fountain had given way to yet more cars.

Within the mall, one thing had changed very little. This was the glass-sided lift, jam-packed with young mothers and their baby buggies. The see-through lift was introduced, in the United States, not because of the view out, but because of the view in. Women, it was argued, would not fear being groped or raped in a glass-sided elevator. Jane Jacobs stated that 'The bedrock of a successful city district is that a person must feel personally safe and secure on the street among all these strangers.' In a mall you meet no alkies, beggars or pickpockets. Shoppers dress up, and smile. Women don't need to wear handbags slung across their chests.

Lakeside had smartened up a bit down the years. I'd guess that the arrival of the Bluewater mall, just across the Thames, and a clear competitor, caused a slight shift upmarket. But the Lakeside pet shop still offered fur-lined cat baskets, toy tigers for the cats to cuddle up to, and two-tier scratching opportunities (pillars wound round with rope and supporting blue velvet cat-napping spots), imported from America. Dogs could have doggy jackets in every size from 10 to 24, mostly tartan.

Lakeside's shoppers included an unnatural percentage of blondes. A stall offered a handsome display of 'human hair extensions' (for 'instant length'): 'You can wash, dry and style it just as you would do your own hair . . . Hair dryer, hot rollers, hot sticks, tongs and other styling equipment.' A girl of about six was having her blonde curls re-styled. An NHS poster in the lavatories asked: 'Have you slept with the love bug? Free chlamydia screening for under-25s.' A tiny chapel was tucked in alongside. A bowl of flowers on the altar table in front of a plain wooden crucifix. The chaplain came every Wednesday between 4 and 6 pm. A blue ceramic postbox awaited 'your prayer requests'. The chapel poster said: 'I am the living water. Come. Drink. Live.'

Once you are inside a mall, it is a wholly pedestrian experience. For you to rest your feet, and spend a bit more money, a boardwalk by Lakeside's lake offered a choice of chain-restaurants. You looked out at pedal boats designed as white or black swans. I noticed a young woman with both little fingers crooked, a manner of eating which I thought had died out. The top-floor Food Court was less fussed about this kind of thing. Burger King asked if you were 'Crying out for onion rings'. Café Giardino offered 'Italian-style meatballs'. Hot & Healthy proposed a 'Fat Jacket' lunch: 'Half a baked potato with Heinz Alphabetti plus Robinsons Fruit Shoot drink.' Kids' price: £2.49.

Almost everyone at Lakeside was at least three inches shorter than me, and I'm not tall. Genetics? Environment? Both?

I drove off down the A13 – the grimmest of radial roads – towards Dagenham. Lakeside has given Basildon a better off-centre town centre than it ever had before. But at Dagenham, the planners never got to creating much of a centre at all. The slogan of the founding fathers of the Becontree estate, which dominates Dagenham, was: houses, houses and more houses. With Becontree the London County Council began to push out towards the new East End. For my Dagenham handbook I brought with me the sociologist Peter Willmott's 1960s study of Becontree. It was the largest of all the LCC's city-edge estates. Willmott claimed that it was the largest housing estate in the world. There are 4 square miles of doggedly similar houses. Officially there were 167,000 inhabitants when the LCC declared the estate complete, in 1935. This was the year that Dagenham's best-known son, the actor and musician Dudley Moore, was born. Even more houses were built later. Almost all the residents were council tenants.

In the estate's heyday, employment came largely from car-making. Ford's Thames-side Dagenham car works was modelled on the firm's elephantine plant at Dearborn, Michigan. Opened in 1930, 'Fordsville', as the locals called it, became the largest industrial works in Europe. By 1953, 40,000 people worked here. In 2002, car production ceased. One of Henry Ford's axioms was that, in his business, nothing was permanent, not even the location. A roadside morass of empty land and empty sheds was the outcome. The houses I saw along the road were run-down and depressed. One was propped up by breeze blocks. A 1930s cinema had become a black church: the Church of Fire and Miracles Ministries. Many black workers were tempted to come to Fordsville. Others have settled here since.

You must never judge a 'community' – that slippery word – by the beauty, or ugliness, of its buildings. Forty years after the first Becontree houses were built, Willmott found that, apparently against the odds, displaced eastenders from Shoreditch or Bethnal Green had recreated a network of neighbourliness. (This was also the lesson of H.J. Gans's study of Levittowns.) But now?

The roads and roundabouts into Dagenham were lined, I saw, with everything a trucker might want, on his way to or from the great docks at Harwich or Felixstowe. Table-dancing at The Circus tavern. Drive-in paint jobs. A farm shop said: 'Get your mince pies [eyes] on these new pots.' But at Dagenham Heathway, near the Underground station, a late-1970s shopping arcade seemed to be dying on its feet. The parking spaces were tattooed all over with tag-writing. One of the hospice charity shops had a white satin wedding dress in the window. There was a Woolworth's, an Iceland, a 'cheque and pawn' shop and a Poundstore: 'everyday items . . . at low prices . . . every day'. Jawoo Foods stocked Caribbean cuts of chicken.

Homes in Dagenham had changed socially since the Willmott survey, for two reasons: first, many tenants had bought their houses from the council, under right-to-buy; secondly, high-paid, if often very repetitive, work at Ford's had almost gone. There was the same social divide in Dagenham that now characterises many zones of what used to be working class Britain. There are the households that still prosper, that have two earners, who live in a house they own. Then there are those households with no earners at all, who live in a house they rent from a local council or a housing association. About half the Becontree tenants bought their homes, usually in the days of well-paid Fordsville jobs. I saw the usual outward signs: the classical pillars, the fancy doors, oriel windows, plastic cladding. All this was a great relief from the previous greyness, with its endless municipal repeat of basic types, details and motifs. A street of new homes had been named Ron Todd Close, after a one-time famously tough union leader. A notice said: 'Private Road'. But those people who couldn't afford to buy their homes, or didn't want to, were stuck in an older Becontree.

Right-to-buy, at strongly subsidised prices, was a policy that began, in a tiny way, in the 1950s. As the offer spread out, it was the greatest-ever gift of wealth to the British working class. The policy's highly vocal opponents got it wrong. In walking around council estates, I have hardly ever met anyone who objected to right-to-buy. What they objected to was the laggardliness in building new homes to rent.

Right-to-buy had one very important after-effect in Dagenham and elsewhere. Council rules prevented sons and daughters settling near their parents. The creation of a local housing market removed those shackles. If they find a buyer, owners can sell to whom they want. I walked into one of Becontree's multitudinous cul-de-sacs. They call them 'banjos' here, because of the turning circle at the end. A hefty east London grandmother stood at one door, watching her daughter unload the grandchildren from a Toyota. A woman came out from another door with her two children to ask – very justifiably – what I was doing. I was counting house-fronts. To judge by appearances, only two out of sixteen remained unsold. You could hardly move for cars.

Turning to go back towards central London, through the school pick-up traffic jam, I found myself facing a huge travel poster. A woman in a strappy swimsuit was sitting on a tropical beach. 'Together,' the caption said, 'we'll go far.' Eastenders no longer stand still.

Shed culture: back gardens at the Becontree estate, Dagenham.

3. THE HISTORY OF A HYSTERIA

Suburbia is a crop that comes in numerous forms, adapting itself to growth and survival in many different places and at many different times. Of recent suburbias, London is the leading-edge example. Los Angeles was, for many years, mocked as a thousand suburbs in search of a city. This was a libel. It was – as the architecture and design critic Reyner Banham spelled out, in a 1971 study – just a new kind of city. Or, more exactly, the ultimate embodiment of a kind of city, which London had pioneered.

London is unimaginable without suburbs. This is one reason why it is so strange for so much of the comment about its present and future to be obsessed with the innermost segments of it. London has for centuries been a multi-centred city. Richard Rogers, a very interesting architect but a much less perceptive urban planner, favoured a new version of a historic wall, with the city built up more densely within it. Under his influence, something like this became public policy in London. By 2006, it was reported, 29 per cent of new homes were being built within the Greater London Authority boundaries on land that used to be someone's garden. This was up from 13 per cent in 1997. It meant less greenery, fewer trees and more big blocks of flats. Rogers is Anglo-Italian by background. His family fled to England in 1938 to get away from the Mussolini regime as it lurched towards war with Britain. He was born in Florence, and he seems always to have made it his yardstick of how a city should be.

Or at least the Florence of an imagined past. The Florence of modern Italy is not quite the city that tourists see. Like many old European cities, it has gone in for a new version of suburbia – call it sprawl if you like – stretching further and further into the former countryside. Florence is not alone. In his social and economic survey *Italy and its Discontents* (2001), Paul Ginsborg speaks of 'the new villas on the peripheries of the small cities of central and northern Italy, complete with their iron railings, their water-sprayed lawns, and flotillas of various-sized cars', where 'the animal spirits of Italian capitalism found their kingdom'. Throughout Italy, 'there has been an inexorable rise in home ownership'. These homes have seldom been in city centres.

By popular vote, bungalows are a design success story. Town and country campaigners loathe them. Opposite: A red-and-white themed version, Frome, Somerset.

Paris is a vivid example of change in a very old city. When you next take the Eurostar train from St Pancras International to the Gare du Nord, look carefully out of the carriage windows at the suburbs you are going past. And if you have taken the car instead, and are driving south through what pass as outer ring roads around Paris, you can hardly escape them. This is the Paris beyond the *péripherique*, the road built around the Paris of the nineteenth century along the line of the old city ramparts. It is a very different city from the tourists' city. One French urban sociologist François Ascher calls today's Paris a 'metapolis', as opposed to a metropolis. The analogy is with metamorphosis, the process whereby a caterpillar becomes a butterfly. In other words, it goes beyond our usual idea of a city.

Within France, the Paris metapolis is a symbol, in steel, concrete and glass, of the nation's recent history. Even as late as the end of the Second World War, France was still a very rural country. In Britain, the population was 80 per cent urban by 1901. But in France, in 1946, only slightly more than half the population lived in towns or cities. Today more than 70 per cent do. Ascher reckons that almost a quarter of these live in the Paris metapolis. And nine out of ten of the French population either live in a town of more than 50,000 people or are within a half-hour drive.

You could, similarly, talk of metapolitan Florence with all its out-of-town villas and subsidiary villages. Once upon a time, as they say in fairy tales, the centre of such a city was the place to be. The closer to the centre the better. Not so, any more, except for some specialised functions. You need to be able to get the airport, the motorway, and of course your suburban home. If you do still live in the old city – surrounded by the density of everyday life so beloved by architects and planners – you need, also, to be able quickly to get somewhere else for the weekend and for national holidays. More and more Italians have second homes. Even during the High Renaissance, Florence was not such a densely built city as it is nostalgically presented to be. In its Medici heyday, Florence never held more than 90,000 people – fewer than modern Colchester. It had more farmland than buildings within its city walls. This was the Medici version of sprawl.

Why did London grow differently? Because, from the end the of the seventeenth-century civil war between royalists and parliamentarians, there was no serious external threat of an attack by land. The city walls had outlived their usefulness, and were demolished. By contrast, for example, the city of Cologne – growing much more slowly, still living in fear of attack, and having quite an amount of farmland within the walls to build on – did not shift its own walls outwards until 1882. As Steen Eiler Rasmussen noted, London just added suburb to suburb.

Even before the walls of London were torn down, the multi-centre model had been launched. The City of London became, more and more, a business centre. The City of Westminster, a mile away, was the administrative centre: court, monarch and eventually parliament. The trading centre versus the political centre. Across the river, to the south, there was already another kind of suburb – the Borough, where all the usual entertainments were corralled: brothels, theatres, taverns. A prototype Las Vegas. As London needed to bolt on locations for new kinds of people or trades, it built more suburbs. Almost everything that is now thought of as the central city was built as a suburb. When railways were first built on the European continent, they were usually thought of as a way to get from city to city. London seized the chance to use them to get from city centre to suburb. Hence the Metropolitan Railway's ultra-suburban 'Metroland'. Again and again John Betjeman returned to his love affair with this pebbledashed stretch of north-west London. By contrast, in his semi-autobiographical first novel, Julian Barnes, who grew up there, has a chapter headed '*J'habite Metroland*'. In it, he evokes his adolescent rejection of suburbia, as opposed to what he saw as the delights of genuinely metropolitan Paris. (But, then, don't all teenagers reject the place they grew up in?)

To begin with, suburbs were, for most people, walking suburbs, in places like the old East End of London (Whitechapel, Wapping, Stepney). This could mean a trudge of several miles. There was a pub every few hundred yards, at least, to cheer the weary, homebound workman on his way. New suburbs were linked to the city centre by new forms of transport. The so-called New Urbanists, led by the Luxemburg-born architect Leon Krier, propose that the new-model city should put everything you need within a ten-minute walk. It is a long time – two centuries? – since this was true. Architecture is often credited with more power than it actually has. Whatever you build, you cannot to push people's freely chosen habits back by 200 years. F.M.L. Thompson described suburbia as 'a state of mind'. A way of life has grown up, and this way of life is suburban.

In an interview, the novelist J.G. Ballard, who lived for fifty years in a west London suburb, said he saw suburbia as the logical subject for a writer seeking to track shifts in culture. As opposed those many writers who seem to think that the London boroughs of Camden, Islington and Kensington & Chelsea represent the whole spectrum of human life. 'It's no accident,' Ballard was quoted as saying, 'that so many postwar cultural trends, like television ownership, video ownership, the transformation of the home into a sort of film studio with all the latest gadgets – it's no coincidence that all this has taken place in the suburbs. People have more money to spend. They can indulge whims.'

His was, for the time being, a rare voice of sympathy and common sense. Panic about suburbia has been building up since at least the early nineteenth century. It was as if the suburb were a wild beast, with a deceptively cosy-looking pelt, which had somehow escaped from control. Admittedly, this freedom from control was a large part of the first attraction of suburbs. In the cheap streets to the east of the City of London, smelly, noxious trades – tanning, brewing, brick-making – could spring up unregulated. But a panic began, in a small way at first, as the suburbs began to grow and grow.

Since the early nineteenth century, almost every anti-suburbia tract has reprinted George Cruikshank's 1829 cartoon, 'The march of bricks and mortar'. He drew this while he sat at his desk in Clerkenwell – itself an earlier suburb – and fretted about all the houses being shoved up wholesale in Camden Town and Islington. This land had been made more accessible by the world's first ever by-pass, the 'New Road', from the City to Paddington. (It has since divided its nomenclature into the Marylebone, Euston, Pentonville and City Roads.) Cruikshank's worry was that there were simply too many of these houses, and that the only gainers were the mostly aristocratic owners of the land, such as the Earl of Camden himself. By the time Dickens wrote *Dombey and Son* in 1847–8, the worries were rather different. The future had arrived in an unexpected guise. The steam train was invented, and the great northbound railway termini all lined up to face the New Road: Euston, St Pancras and King's Cross. The works to build these lines crammed more and more people into the houses they left undemolished. Dickens, who had lived for a while as a child in Camden Town, knew the social outcome all too well. Not even the dead were safe. To build the line into St Pancras, corpses were exhumed from the old St Pancras churchyard. (This was one of Thomas Hardy's first jobs as an apprentice architect. I have

always suspected that the gloom of the task seeped into his novels.) Many of the remaining corpses were shifted more recently, when St Pancras was re-shaped to become the London terminus of the Eurostar trains to Paris.

The dirt and din from the steam engines pulled all the nearby suburbs down in the world. When Trollope's hero Paul Montague, in *The Way We Live Now* (1874–5), goes to Islington from his mother's Marylebone house to visit Mrs Hurtle, the mistress he has dumped, he makes it very clear that he is going two or three steps down, socially, even though Marylebone itself was fairly shabby-genteel by then.

The suburbs are never as settled as they seem. When the steam trains gave way to diesel and electric traction, those once-derided inner suburbs started their inexorable climb back into fashion. Upper Street, Islington, for example, is now lined with shops and restaurants that would have been unimaginable without customers from the newly restored Georgian houses, who were dripping in City money. In his autobiography *Interesting Times*, the historian

Eric Hobsbawm recounts how, not long after the Second World War, he and his wife moved into a flat in Gloucester Crescent in Camden Town. A few years later, a literary enclave came together in this street, including the theatre director Jonathan Miller, the playwrights Alan Bennett and Michael Frayn, and the biographer Claire Tomalin. A fashionable cartoonist Mark Boxer based a chic comic strip, 'The Stringalongs', on life in the crescent. It had evolved into a smart high-bohemian address. But to the twenty-eight-year-old Hobsbawm in 1946, newly demobilised from his wartime tasks as a sergeant in the Pioneer Corps, it was 'the western outpost of the vast zone of London's bombed and yet totally ungentrified East End'. It was cheap, and handy for buses to the British Museum reading room.

No one would now call Gloucester Crescent 'East End'. And the tide of gentrification has since swept ever eastwards. Islington was undeniably East-End-ish until at least the 1960s. Now, even parts of Hackney and Bethnal Green have moved psychologically, if not geographically, towards the West End. London has become increasingly professional-class. The Georgian and Victorian houses that such families would like to inhabit are what economists call a 'positional good'. No one is manufacturing them any more. To catch a suitable home, you must throw your fishing line ever further out. You may even, one day, have to re-appreciate the charms of the much despised interwar semi. In London, almost every white van outside a gentrifying house – the builder, the plumber, the electrician, the kitchen fitter, the garden designer – carries an address in Essex, Hertfordshire or Kent. The families of nearly all craftsmen have already made that move outward.

The early twentieth-century suburban growth that, in London, produced the greatest panic, was helped along by rail commuter lines and, above all, by the Underground. The Tube pierced out into cheap agricultural land. The Underground's owners buttressed the network's profits by property deals and by selling commuter tickets to the owners of all the brand-new houses. The greatest Tube expansionists were American. Charles Tyson Yerkes, a huckster and fraudster, unified and electrified the early Underground. Later, the American-trained Albert Stanley, Lord Ashfield, Derbyshire-born and Detroit-educated, moved back to England from running New Jersey's transit system. With his general manager Frank Pick, Ashfield oversaw the Tube's deepest extension into untouched countryside. The greatest suburban boom was in the 1920s and

1930s, in a potent combination of cheap building costs and cheap mortgages, offered by the thriving building societies.

There was a change of attitude. More and more families wanted privacy and greenery, in place of a crowded terrace or flat in the inner city. The new estates of council houses, as at Becontree, purveyed a cut-price, less successful variant: a bastard version of Ebenezer Howard's garden city dream. There was also, and perhaps more importantly, a change in the kinds of job. The factories of companies making radios, vacuum cleaners and washing machines stretched out along the Great West Road, the Great Cambridge Road and Eastern Avenue, the new arterial roads out of London. The car makers were at Luton (Vauxhall) and Cowley (Morris), as well as Dagenham. The entire pull was centrifugal.

But what was to become of Old England? The man asking the question most forcefully was an architect called Clough Williams-Ellis. Or, to be precise, Williams-Ellis and his wife Amabel, one of the powerful Strachey clan of Bloomsbury intellectuals. She did most of the writing, though the books appeared in her husband's sole name. His own best-known architecture consists of an Italian toy village, Portmeirion, on the north Wales coast, much used as a holiday destination by other left-wing intellectuals. In 1928, the Williams-Ellises published *England and the Octopus*. The octopus was suburbia. Nine years later, in 1937, they published *Britain and the Beast*. The beast was the bungalow.

The Williams-Ellises mourned that change had been so violent, since the 1914–18 world war ended, that 'the thoughtful among us ... sadly wonder whether anything recognisable of our lovely England will be left for our children's children'. The trouble, as they saw it, was the spread of 'mean and petty little houses that surely none but mean and petty little souls should inhabit with satisfaction'. In the attack on the new suburbia, the tinge of snobbery sets in early. Why aren't these upstarts satisfied with the crowded terraces and tenements of the past?

THIS BUNGALOW BUILT ANYWHERE for £145 including Foundations DEPOSIT ONLY £15

Timber framed and asbestos bungalows built anywhere to your own design. Small extra charge for exterior in brickwork.
Write for free illustrated catalogue to—
THOMPSON, BAYLISS & Co. Ltd., DEPT. 50, RAINHAM, ESSEX.

Choose your Site— we will buy it for you. Repayments on easy terms.

This Modern 4-Roomed Bungalow as shown at the IDEAL HOME EXHIBITION, OLYMPIA

Housing off the peg: 1936 advertisement.

The onward march of the bungalows. They featured as 'the Beast' in Clough Williams-Ellis's influential polemic, Britain and the Beast (1937). Top row, left to right: Moreton, Essex; Berkeley, Gloucestershire; prefab, Lewisham, south London; Craigleith, Edinburgh. Middle row, left to right: Lyme Regis, Dorset; Roxwell, Essex (called Barrymore, probably after the film star); Kingswood, Surrey; Bingley, west Yorkshire; Bottom row, left to right: Wellington, Herefordshire; Walton-on-the-Naze, Essex; Glastonbury, Somerset.

The Williams-Ellis duo were, undeniably, fierce and entertaining polemicists:

> Take any square mile you like of semi-urban Black Country or of the industrial North or Midlands or the outer suburbs of almost any town – or take Peacehaven [on the Sussex coast], Waterlooville [outside Portsmouth] or Bournemouth, or an up-to-date Ordnance Survey map of the same areas. It is difficult to believe that the houses have been deliberately placed just *so* by thinking social animals – an untutored and charitable Martian would surely deride the idea, and suggest the more likely theory that the buildings had been caught by some tidy-minded wizard playing unauthorised blind-man's-buff in a bit of no-man's-land, and had been punished for their skittishness by being petrified on the instant, just wherever they happened to stand.

There was great anguish among architects and would-be planners at something burgeoning so merrily that was completely outside their control. The threat had been there for a long time. In his architectural history of London, Anthony Sutcliffe notes that, as the city began its headlong nineteenth-century expansion, architects backed off. The job of building all those new terraces was trade, not art. (There were few modest semis then, though John Nash had already designed some precursors: neo-classical semi-detached houses at the edge of Regent's Park.) 'After 1830 architects gradually withdrew from development and builders took their place,' Sutcliffe wrote. These men could work 'on the bigger scale that London now demanded'. Some used architects, especially for estates like Belgravia, which aspired to high fashion. But many did not. London spilled out north and north-east, where residents could make use of the new railways for going to work. The developers found, as Sutcliffe reports, that 'there were people of genteel aspirations such as teachers, doctors and solicitors who appreciated a superior environment'. If suburbia was a beast, it had been preparing to spring for a long time. The urban historian H.J. Dyos detected a noticeable 'suburban trend' from the 1860s, which became even more marked from the 1880s.

The onrush of semis began around 1900, with their watered-down, but usually well-built, versions of Voysey's cottagey designs and Baillie Scott's half-timbering. '"Mon Ami" stares vacantly at the shameful hinder parts of "Loch

Lomond", ' the Williams-Ellises write, 'which in turn is overlooked and put out of countenance by the baleful scowl of "Kia-Ora" on its flank.' The revulsion begins to seem almost Freudian: what is all this about 'hinder parts' and a 'baleful scowl'? It's undeniable that the quiet privacy of suburbia has always led to the assumption of mysterious temptations. Brothels discovered in the suburbs always get bigger headlines than brothels in the middle of Soho. The best known was Cynthia Payne's 'House of Cyn' in Streatham (later made into the 1987 film *Personal Services*). But the *Guardian*, for example, was excited in 2008 to find a thriving Chinese-staffed brothel in the even more genteel suburb of Cheam. The wife swapping, intermittently 'exposed' by the Sunday papers, always seems to take place behind neat hedges and well-mown lawns. The 1970s porn star Mary Millington (*née* Mary Ruth Quilter) was born in Kenton. Her fan club's website maintains that she combined the charms of a 'girl next door' with those of a 'sex superstar'.

Bedford Park, begun 1877, was architect-designed. It is one of the few suburbs that architecture writers applaud.

The novel *Suburban Souls* was published around 1901, and reprinted by Wordsworth Editions in 1995 in its 'Classic Erotica' series. It consists entirely of Jacky S., the forty-ish narrator, taking the train out of town, nominally to have tea with the Arvel family, but really to try to seduce the nineteen-year-old daughter, Lily, in her 'suburban paradise', where she lives with her father, mother and brother. The narrator discovers, to his delight but eventual suspicion, that the supposedly virginal Lily needs little tuition in depravity. Many of the goings-on take place in the first-class compartment of the commuter train. The editors of the new edition note, perhaps too solemnly, that the novel was probably first published in the same year as Freud's *The Psychopathology of Everyday Life*.

Clough Williams-Ellis, as an architect, was plunged into his deepest gloom by the ready-made aspect of much suburban building. He and Amabel ended *England and the Octopus* with a reproduction of an advertisement for 'The Cottabunga'. Messrs Brown and Lily, of Reading, announced: 'This charming bungalow cottage delivered, carriage paid, to any goods station in England and Wales, ready to erect, for £245: 10 nett.' And the firm claimed: 'Cottabunga buildings may be seen dotted all over the Countryside, North-East-South-West, and are giving universal

satisfaction.' The houses' gables were, of course, half-timbered.

By the time of *Britain and the Beast*, the well-connected Williams-Ellises were beginning to get support from other members of the Establishment. This collection of polemical essays by various authors came with endorsements from the former Liberal Prime Minister Lloyd George, the former Labour leader George Lansbury, the Minister of Health Kingsley Wood and the biologist Julian Huxley. The essayists included the economist J.M. Keynes, the pop philosopher C.E.M. Joad, the historian G.M. Trevelyan and the biologist and planner Patrick Abercrombie. By now the battle was half-won. The London County Council would get its Green Belt Act through parliament in 1938. Wider green belt and central planning powers would follow in 1947, under a government in which Amabel Williams-Ellis's brother John Strachey was a leading cabinet minister.

The 'By-Pass Variegated' style. Brilliantly evoked by Osbert Lancaster in his cartoon history of architecture, Pillar to Post, *1938. He forecast that such estates 'will inevitably become the slums of the future'. Prediction is always hazardous.*

Many of the essayists were ferocious. In 'Lessons from Other Countries', Lord Howard of Penrith praised a Nazi law of 26 June 1935 on preserving natural beauty: 'a model for the rest of the world'. But a design writer, John Gloag, introduced an intriguing note of mild dissent in his essay, 'The Suburban Scene'. He did not completely disagree with the critics, he said, but he acknowledged that socially 'an unacknowledged revolution is in full swing'. 'I am not making a plea for the retention of those repellent jerry-built, sham-Tudor houses that disfigure England; but I do suggest that the reason why people are happy in them, why they can take pride in them, is worth studying. You can't impose theories of living on the English.' (In fact, few, if any, were jerry-built.) Gloag thought that the fiercest critics were probably all fans of the Modern movement. He proposed that they should 'travel occasionally in crowded third-class carriages in the bowler-hat hours; and then let them listen to the gardening chatter that seeps under the newspaper barriers that every man erects against a possible neighbour, until he recognises a garden-lover.' The choices, the freedoms, of suburbia were unappreciated by the anti-suburbanites, Gloag wrote: 'The Englishman is always having some little experiments thrust upon him. His pleasures are curbed; his life is interfered with in little pettifogging ways.'

The Williams-Ellises were not alone in demonising the suburbs. In reading novels or poetry of the early twentieth century, you find it is part of the small change of conversation. It is as common – though less disconcerting to us now – as mild anti-semitism. In *The Thirty-Nine Steps* (1915), the hero Richard Hannay claims to see the suburbs as home to a race apart:

> A man of my sort, who has travelled about the world in rough
> places, gets on perfectly well with two classes, what you may call
> the upper and the lower. I was at home with herds and tramps and
> roadmen, and I was sufficiently at ease with men like Sir Walter
> [permanent secretary at the Foreign Office] and the men I had
> met the night before. I can't explain why, but it is a fact. But what
> fellows like me don't understand is the great comfortable, satisfied
> middle class world, the folk that live in villas and suburbs. He
> doesn't know how they look at things, he doesn't understand their
> conventions, and he is as shy of them as of a black mamba.

The hero of P.G. Wodehouse's novel *Big Money* (1931) has to take to suburbia temporarily, in pursuit of riches and romance. He sees the suburbs as less a threat than a big adventure:

> With his usual masterful dash in the last fifty yards Berry Conway
> had beaten the 8.45 express into Valley Fields station by the
> split-second margin which was his habit. Alien though he felt
> the suburbs were to him, he possessed in a notable degree that
> gift which marks off suburbanites from other men – the uncanny
> ability to catch a train and never to catch it by more than three and
> a quarter seconds.

Wodehouse was, by this date, comfortably settled in the United States, with a profitable line in writing stories for the *Saturday Evening Post* and libretti for Broadway musicals. But he knew all about 'Valley Fields', which is clearly based on the south London suburb of Dulwich where he went to school. He also, I'm sure, knew where most of his British readers lived: in suburbia.

In Graeme Greene's short story 'A Drive in the Country' (1937), the heroine's father is head clerk at an export agency. Through 'the thin wall of the jerry-built villa', she can hear the voices in other rooms, and even the 'dim sounds of tenderness and comfort between the two middle-aged strangers' – her mother and father, in the next room. 'In fifteen years, she thought unhappily, the house will be his; he had paid twenty-five pounds down and the rest he was paying month by month as rent. "Of course," he was in the habit of saying after a good meal, "I've improved the property . . . If we had to sell now we should get back more than I've paid from the society".' His especial joy was the garden: 'A pile of bricks,' he would say, 'that's all it was.'

Winifred Watson's bestselling novel *Miss Pettigrew Lives for a Day* (1938), reads like the script for a Mayfair-based Fred Astaire movie (and in 2008, Hollywood filmed it). Poor provincial Miss Pettigrew, who has spent her life, very dimly, as a governess or paid companion, finds herself giving marital advice to a West End part-time actress and full-time floozie whose stage name is Delysia LaFosse (birth name Sarah Grubb). There are three well-to-do contenders for an engagement ring: Phil Goldberg, a potential backer for Delysia's next play; Nick Caldarelli, who is already paying the rent for her Knightsbridge flat; and Michael, who loves her, but occasionally beats her, and whose father is a wholesaler of fish. Phil and Nick are already sleeping with her, and Michael may be (the details are unclear). To Miss Pettigrew's mind, the trouble with Michael is easily explained:

> And this good young man, this Michael, who wants to marry you, has all the virtues, but he's dull. He has no fire . . . no imagination. He

In Ian Nairn's polemic, Outrage (1955), he called suburbia 'Subtopia.' This drawing, he said, showed 'the effect of several agents of Subtopia acting in concert'. Nairn's illustrator was Gordon Cullen, whose ideal townscape was Brixham harbour, Devon. Cullen's influence explains the cobble patches and bollards in subsequent street designs.

would stifle your spirit. You want colour, life, music. He would offer you a . . . a house in suburbia.

She sees this as the clincher. But in due course the charming Phil is dropped: specifically, he's too Jewish. The ultra-sexy Nick is also dropped: too Italian. So Michael it finally is – 'he's *all* English' – even though his father's money does come from a chain of fish shops. He is 'a Hercules of a man: a Clark Gable of a man'. Delysia LaFosse prepares herself to leave the Knightsbridge flat. She spells it out:

> You see, Michael has a kink. He will live in a big house with big rooms. He says he spent all his youth with a family of nine all cooped up in a little flat with the walls closing in on him and never a room to himself, and He Will Have Space.

Michael has his eye on an immense house already – no doubt in the stockbroker belt of suburban Surrey or in the north London equivalent, Totteridge. But (Miss LaFosse reports): 'He says even if he does marry me, he still wants, he still wants a comfortable home and I'm a rotten housekeeper.' So poor, downtrodden, never-been-kissed Miss Pettigrew takes the job of keeping house, while beginning to have high hopes of her new 'beau', Joe Bloomfield, whom she meets at the Mayfair nightclub (owned by Nick) where Delysia LaFosse sometimes sings. Joe's money comes from the corset trade. End of story. It sounds to me as though suburbia was victorious. As it happens, the corset trade is what saved the world's first-ever garden city, Letchworth, from economic collapse. Spirella opened a factory there. Letchworth is really a planned suburb in the Hertfordshire countryside, the precursor of Welwyn Garden City and the postwar New Towns.

Those were the kinds of settlement William-Ellis, as an architect, approved of. He praised Welwyn Garden City, and after the Second World War he was appointed as chairman of the Stevenage New Town development corporation. Following his lead, the only suburbs the architectural profession has ever favoured are those built by architects: Bedford Park and Brentham in west London, the garden cities, Hampstead Garden Suburb and the New Towns.

Orwell differed. He disliked the new suburbia west of London, but he had little time for Letchworth, either. He lived near by, in Wallington, a tiny village where he was trying to add to his earnings, or at least limit his outgoings, by running a village shop.

*Hampstead Garden Suburb, founded
in 1906, is architect-designed, hence
architect-approved. Most inhabitants
move here for spaciousness and foliage,
rather than the detail of house design.
Intended for 'artisans' as well as the
middle classes, it now reveals little or
no evidence of the former group.*

I found you could buy a copy of Orwell's marriage certificate in the Wallington village church, for £2, and a postcard of his cottage for 50p. The year after he married Eileen O'Shaunessy in Wallington on 6 June 1936 was the happiest of his life. The two of them opened up the general store that a previous tenant had given up as a bad job. Here Orwell wrote *The Road to Wigan Pier* and *Homage to Catalonia*.

Since then, I found, as in much of the English countryside, a revolution had taken place. No one was about. The village – a hamlet, really – was dead. I saw one man tinkering with his car. I had come to Wallington through the wet, misty, yearning Hertfordshire countryside. I passed the damp flags of a village fête and a pub called The Moon and Star. I wondered if this had inspired Orwell's famous essay on the perfect English pub, which he called The Moon Under Water. (The founder of the J.D. Wetherspoon chain of pubs said he took this essay as his inspiration.) There was no general store in Wallington now, no post office – though a house, with a bright blue door, was called The Old Post Office. Nor was there a pub – though one house, with pretty, yellow-flowering jasmine, was called The Old Plough, and another was Derby Arms Cottage.

The church came close to the Betjemanesque ideal of a parish church: elderly wooden pews between whitewashed walls; a Victorian hand-organ; memorial slabs for the Blow and Bowles families dating back to the fifteenth century. The man before me in the guest book, as I signed, was Mr Otelchenko from Minsk (comment: 'Very nice!!!').

In its way, Wallington has come up in the world. To put it another way: it has been suburbanised. On the church postcard, the Orwells' former cottage has a tiled roof. In their day it had a tin roof and an outdoor privy. It now looked to be newly thatched. I walked down a little track marked, officially, as a public footpath. The side of the path was lined with young, suburbanite *leylandii* trees, which would eventually make sure you couldn't overlook the owner's garden. Over a stile I found myself alone with the rooks in a field of rough pasture. The Orwells themselves were forerunners – like Virginia and Leonard Woolf in deepest Sussex – of what happened to the countryside as agricultural work declined. R.E. Pahl wrote a sociological study of 'the two-class village', based on his own observations in Hertfordshire. He called his book *Urbs in Rure* ('Town in the Country'). He noted how the new arrivals, most of them commuters, and full of the spirit of 'community', gradually took over the running of every village they came to. The locals went into internal exile. (I noticed the same process in

Hebden Bridge from the 1970s on.) It looked clear who had won, right across Hertfordshire. The county was so handy for London. It was also reported to have a higher concentration of IT jobs than any other shire. Rural villages are one-class again, as they were as late as the 1930s, but it is a different class. After the monoculture of the farms comes the monoculture of culture.

That Saturday, everyone was off shopping. Orwell used to catch the bus into Letchworth. I went the same way, though I suspected that most of the car-drivers of Wallington had gone the other, more stylish way, into Cambridge, with its town-edge ring of Tesco, Waitrose and the rest.

Letchworth's creator Ebenezer Howard was a practical-minded futurist. He was very influenced by some years he had spent in Chicago. He admired Americans' get-up-and-go, their suspicion of central government, and the spaciousness of the way they lived. He thought you would never get anywhere if you waited for governments to take up a new idea. Hence Letchworth: 3,918 acres bought by First Garden City (itself a company title with a very American tone) from fifteen farm owners at £40.75 an acre. Letchworth's neat brick houses launched a thousand council estates. One result is that Letchworth itself now looks like a vast council estate: the style is so trademarked, socially. Howard's chief architects were two brothers-in-law, Raymond Unwin and Barry Parker. Together, Unwin and Parker went on to design Hampstead Garden Suburb. Parker, solo, designed Wythenshawe, Manchester Corporation's town-edge version of the Becontree estate (Some call it England's third garden city, after Letchworth and Welwyn.) Unwin, Parker and Howard's principles inspired Britain's cluster of New Towns, from Stevenage (the first) to Milton Keynes (the biggest). As my bus juddered in, Letchworth proudly displayed its primacy as First Garden City on roadside placards.

The road from Wallington had taken me past the usual retail-park array: Homebase, Halfords and the rest. The business park housed a busy Sainsbury's. Letchworth's main street had had a Morrison's store inserted among a cluster of cheap shops and charity outlets. Next to a McDonalds, a one-man bandsman, dressed in a union jack, played 'Walking Through a Winter Wonderland', on drums, cymbals, mouth organ, tambourine and klaxon. If a place is ever going to look lively, it will be on a Saturday afternoon. But, for all Letchworth's status as a pioneer of planning, I could have been in a run-down ex-industrial northern town like Sunderland or Barnsley. The pervading look was of a depressed shabbiness. People had pallid, weary faces. Many of the women smoked. Clothes looked old and cheap. One mother was taking her two small, pink-clad daughters into the Help the Aged store in search of bargains. Everyone looked as if they were in minimum-wage jobs or on welfare payments, or both.

Letchworth tried to build a vision of the future. The trouble with the future is that it never stays still. You arrive and find it's not there. The town had two main employers: Spirella, who pioneered factory work in Letchworth, and the British Tabulating-Machine Company, pioneers of punched-card calculators. The last time I was in the Letchworth local museum it displayed the scroll given to the members of BTC's Majority Club. You joined this if you worked with the company for twenty-one years. (After forty-two years you became a Double Majority member, and got an inscribed silver bowl.) The museum also had naughty postcards of early Spirella models, bending over in front of long mirrors, with lots of white lace. Both firms went. BTC was killed by computers. The Spirella works has been rejigged as offices, within its charming Arts & Crafts exterior, in the hope of regeneration. The museum, meanwhile, had switched its display to birds and trees.

Orwell mocked Letchworth for its sandals-and-nuts socialism. His hostility permeates Part Two of *The Road to Wigan Pier*. 'One sometimes gets the impression that the mere words "Socialism" and "Communism" draw towards them with magnetic force every fruit-juice drinker, nudist, sandal-wearer, sex maniac, Quaker, "Nature Cure" quack, pacifist and feminist in England.' Anyone who set about re-drafting the mission statements of European socialist parties in the past twenty years, in order to insert a touch of environmentalism, will blench at this scornful list. Letchworth was New Age before its time. But the lavish headquarters of the Theosophical Society, Madam Blavatsky's eccentric, pantheistic sect, is now a masonic lodge. The heart has gone out of Letchworth. No one I talked to, that day or afterwards, could quite explain to me why this was. Could the moral be that jobs matter more than the design of buildings?

As I left Letchworth, I saw a choice of 'folk guitars' in a music shop. Dreams, the bed superstore, offered me 50 per cent off thousands of items – 'guaranteed cheapest beds in Letchworth'. I resisted both temptations, and walked on by.

The world's first garden city, Letchworth, Hertfordshire, founded in 1903. Orwell derided its 'sandals-and-nuts socialism'. The Settlement was built as The Skittles temperance inn in 1907. It became an adult education centre.

Suburbia is about jobs, not just houses. Opposite above: Spirella corset factory, Letchworth, built in 1912–22, brought local work to the garden city. It included a library and ballroom for workers (mainly women), and is now offices. Opposite below: Hoover factory, Great West Road, Perivale, west London (1931–35). Attacked in 1951 by Pevsner as 'perhaps the most offensive of the modernistic atrocities along this road of typical bypass factories', it is now seen as an Art Deco classic. It has been converted to a supermarket and offices. This page, above: Motorola electronics factory, Swindon, Wiltshire (1998), now used for research and development. Left: Victorian mill in Bingley, west Yorkshire, a Bradford exurb. It is now the head office of Damart thermal underwear.

73

4. ARCADIA FOR ALL

The poet laureate of the self-help settlements, which Clough and Amabel Williams-Ellis took such a violent dislike to, is the gentle anarchist Colin Ward. The author of many books, he is an unsung prophet in the wider world. Architects and planners pay homage to him, but to follow his precepts would mean abandoning most of the way they work, so the admiration doesn't go much beyond that. Ward is a persistent admirer of all the things that people have managed to do for themselves in the countryside, in spite of all condemnation and regulation. Until the mid-twentieth century, of course, there were very few regulations. One driving force behind the planning system, which was introduced from 1947 onwards, was to stop any such self-help in its tracks. It was untidy, unplanned and so, probably, immoral.

A drastic depopulation of the English countryside began in the late nineteenth century, as agriculture collapsed under the pressure of cheap wheat from Canada, cheap frozen beef from Argentina or Uruguay and cheap frozen lamb from New Zealand. The shacks of the so-called plotlands, and the spaced-out bungalows of new estates, were one way to bring a population back to the countryside. The eventual outcry was much the same as that which now swells up against the caravans of New Age travellers, the settlements of 'mobile homes' or the makeshift residences of urban squatters. (Ward always defended squatters as one way of making authority realise that housing pressure was becoming intense.) The patronising abuse in the early twenty-first century often borrows its language from the United States: 'trailer trash', for example, and 'white trash'. This, it seemed, was the only ethnic group that liberals felt they could publicly disparage.

The analogy with America existed from the start. It was not only in Ireland that the United States was regarded as an exit route from misery and into freedom. After his experiments with a kind of cooperative factory village at New Lanark in Ayrshire in the late eighteenth century – more of a benevolent dictatorship, really – Robert Owen left for America to carry the message further afield by founding the township of New Harmony. This was a failure. But many industrial towns and villages were inspired to emulate Owen. Workers came

Opposite: Self-build home at Jaywick Sands, Clacton-on-Sea. In the 1960s, the Essex coast was a site for pirate radio stations. Pirate planning also flourished here. Or you could call it Non-Plan.

together in the beginnings of the cooperative movement (the Rochdale Pioneers opened their first shop in 1847) and in mutual saving through the early building societies. Hence the little rows of 'club houses' on some Pennine hillsides. Many workers also joined local America Clubs, where the point was to build up funds in order to emigrate.

The landscape of self-help homes in Britain immediately evoked America, as Colin Ward notes in *Arcadia for All*. This extraordinary book combines assiduous research with a fervent advocacy of popular choice. The cover of the 2004 reprint shows two women skipping along the Essex beach at Jaywick Sands. This was one of the settlements most regularly condemned by those who could easily afford their own ready-built homes. These vociferous opponents of self-help probably rented, rather than bought. Well into the twentieth century, the desire to own your home was snobbishly perceived as a phenomenon of aspiring artisans or clerks, obsessed with bettering themselves and the their families. The criticisms were seldom applied if you were an actual aristocrat, in which case land-owning was what you did.

Under the fierce eye of the planners, 'the legacy of a makeshift landscape' – Ward's description – has been steadily whittled away. But the legacy is not extinguished. My own eyes having been opened by Ward, I feel a tug of pleasure when, at such derided villages as Polzeath, in north Cornwall, I see the clear outline of an old railway carriage in the structure of a bungalow near the beach. Such carriages, bought cheap after the rail firms had done with them, were a favourite way to kick-start a makeshift home.

Selsey, west Sussex: a favourite way to create a home on a cheap 'plotlands' site was to buy an old railway carriage. The origins are visible beneath later extensions.

John Betjeman spent his childhood holidays at polite Trebetherick, a couple of miles along the coast from Polzeath, and is buried there. He hated the robust vulgarities of Polzeath with a deep passion. It was created by the car and the caravan. There was never a railway station. One of Betjeman's many quirks was that he claimed to love trains and hate cars, but his affectionate handbook on Cornwall – excoriating Polzeath – appeared in the 'Shell Guide' series, published by the oil company. The fact that Polzeath has now become a centre of the surf-riding boom, complete with bars and beach bums, makes it even more American in feel than it always was. The little valley going inland from Polzeath is solid with caravans.

I went to Jaywick Sands and Peacehaven, its Channel coast cousin, as a sort of pilgrim. I was seeking out Colin Ward's vision of a past that might have lessons for today's future. Jaywick Sands is on the Essex outskirts of Clacton-on-Sea. Peacehaven is on the Sussex outskirts of Brighton.

To fuel my journey to Jaywick, I bought some cockles from Tubby Isaacs's kiosk outside Clacton pier. It was a homage to my Blackpool childhood holidays. Picking the cockles out of their plastic box with a wooden prong, I then set off west, along the Clacton front, towards Jaywick. Clacton itself is Stepney-by-the-Sea. On the streets, boys with gelled hair and footballer T-shirts mingled with retired east Londoners, shopping. Not many 't's or 'th's in Clacton voices. In among the estate agents on Station Road, the sandwich bar was called Roll Wiv It. The jewellery shop was Wot-A-Gem, with the wives-and-girlfriends (of footballers) initials highlighted. A two-bedroom bungalow at Jaywick was advertised at £136,995. Most of the prices ended in 995, like a street market that tempts you to think that 99p is a big improvement on £1.

At the Princes Theatre you could take in smirking Roy 'Chubby' Brown, 'the most outrageous comedian in the world', advertised with the warning 'If easily offended, please stay away'. Or else stony-faced Jim Davidson, portrayed with demonic horns on the poster for his comedy show, *The Devil Rides Out Live*: 'Adults only'. At Clacton postcards were still saucy. A

Jaywick Sands by the sea. DIY heaven. Below: Sign on the side of a house. Middle: A trellis arch over a garden gate. Bottom: The main street.

butcher stood behind his counter in a blue-striped apron. An elderly woman looked in alarm at his display. On either side lay dark heaps of sausages with their different price tags. Directly in front of the butcher, at groin level, a single pale sausage lay on the counter, marked 'Free'. Another card showed two men chatting on the prom. One said to the other: 'Your little brother has filled out after his operation.' They were both staring at a cheerful blonde, bursting out of her bikini. A cartoonist called Terry Irvine, who seemed to have taken over where Donald McGill left off, had signed many of the cards. The pier itself was consolingly noisy. A 20p-in-the-slot machine gave you 'Harry Corbett's Sooty TV Concert' (sax, drums, piano). A 'Dumbo' ride offered flying pink elephants. The 'Paratrooper' ride offered 'the experience of skydiving'. An agency offered holiday caravans from £4,995, along with insurance policies, 'protecting your investment'.

I went on towards Jaywick. The sand was nailed to the beach by a long line of timber groynes. The North Sea was grey-blue, and as flat as the Essex landscape. The deckchair men had opened up their stores. The beach was filling up. A Punch and Judy show was set up, but not yet operating. There were a few beach huts. The interiors were a Vermeer or Pieter de Hooch for our time: families with fridge, stove, basket chairs, Thermos, sandwich materials. I reached a Martello tower, squat and ugly. Here Billy Butlin used to have his holiday camp. All had vanished. In its place was a brick-built estate of houses and flats. The owners of houses next to the sea wall had given almost all of them names: Sea Frieze, Sea Moon, Moonbeam Cottage, Sundaze, Briny Vista, Casa de Mar. The balconies were ablaze with geraniums.

I went on, past a second Martello tower, and here was Jaywick Sands. About 4,000 people lived here, I was told, in what *Arcadia for All* calls 'the largest and most spectacular plotlands settlement on the Essex coast'. It was created by Frank Stedman, a surveyor. He bought several hundred acres of reclaimed marshland in 1928. He then found it was almost impossible to put in proper drains (something not resolved for forty years). So he sold the site off for holiday chalets and beach huts. In the 1930s, a plot 20 feet wide and 30 feet deep went for £30. Bit by bit, ingenious Cockney owners turned their huts into houses.

I could see the lineaments of the old huts – like evidence of the old face underneath the cosmetic surgeon's art – within the bungalows that had swelled out to fill an entire plot. Extra rooms and roofs stuck out at odd angles. At the

Mixed messages at Jaywick: welcome and beware. Cockney friendliness alongside Cockney chippiness. Every house makes its statement. The overall effect is of beach-edge California or Australia. But street names like Hillman, Morris, Humber and Wolseley Avenues evoke days when there really was a British car industry.

cracked corner of one wall, I could make out the construction: wooden planking, overlaid with iron mesh and cement, overlaid with pebbledash skin.

The townscape reminded me of beach-edge California, like Polzeath, or perhaps Australia. But this being England, I found that Jaywick had its 'good' side (traditionally built bungalows away from the sea, where they preferred to call themselves 'West Clacton'), its middling side (floral street names and bungalows that almost conceal their wooden origins) and its rough side. You could have filmed here an Essex version of Hyacinth Bucket and her TV quest to keep up appearances.

One sea-edge house advertised a two bedroom flat to let: 'Workers only'. Many Jaywick residents live on welfare benefits. Every house made its statement: Hunky-Dory, Happy Returns, Why Worry, Bodgers Rest. Love Shack had a cement cat chasing a mouse on its little gable end. Moonbeam was ablaze with flowers: peonies, marigolds, sunflowers, plastic as well as live. A plaque on the gate said: 'Lost dog. Blind in one eye. Missing right ear. Tail broken. Recently castrated. Answers to name of Lucky.'

The roughest neighbourhood was the oldest: 'Brooklands', named after the car-racing circuit. It was laid out with street names that were a paean of praise to the early days of the British car industry: Hillman, Morris, Alvis, Talbot, Humber, Crossley and Wolseley Avenues. Today they sounded more like a funeral dirge. One entire front garden was occupied by a highly polished Ford Mustang tourer. A parked van belonged to 'RDC Promotions for Banger Racing', and old bangers, driven at speed, passed me as I turned into Brooklands. There was a car boot sale where the old boating lake had been tarmacked over. The men walked with a roll from the shoulders as if they were used to heavy lifting.

Jaywick has third-generation families by now, even fourth-generation. Attempts at compulsory demolition had failed. The Guinness Trust housing association had built forty new houses and bungalows behind Brooklands. 'Outsiders might look at the place and say, "Why do they live here?"' the man from the trust said. 'But they are very proud people, with strong views.' Some might want to self-build new homes. He said the trust would encourage this: it was the Jaywick way.

'Some people are living in appalling conditions,' he acknowledged. Visually, all the trust's efforts had made little difference, I thought. A shopkeeper put it another way: 'The place is full of no-hopers who are no use to you.' (But then where are no-hopers supposed to live?) Housing benefit, twelve months of the year, pays much better than summer lets. Some absentee owners had gone off to Spain, leaving chalets vulnerable to arson. I saw that three had been recently burned down. 'Anyway, who wants to come here, rather than the Costa del Sol?' the shopkeeper said. 'Out there your pounds will buy you lots more lager.' Or used to.

A young woman with a baby was one of the third generation. She had come back to Jaywick Sands to rent, after a couple of years away. 'It's *not* your own house, but it *is* your own house. It's a community. You know everyone. We've had a bit of trouble here, but you feel the kids are safe.' The sea was going bluer under the sun. A few people had come out with cans of white paint. Better, I

Two bungalows at Jaywick facing out to the North Sea. The road is called Brooklands, after the Surrey car racing circuit.

Peacehaven on the Sussex coast, east of Brighton. Originally called New Anzac-on-Sea, offering cheap homes for First World War heroes.

thought, to be hard up in shabby, friendly Jaywick than in the destroyed streets of east London.

If you want to give apoplexy to a group outing of architects or planners, I recommend you take them on the No. 11 bus back from Brooklands to Clacton town centre. You go through a sun-forest of small bungalows: avenue after avenue. The boat in a front garden is called Wot 4. You reach open fields: bargain-price golf, a light-aircraft landing strip, the visiting Great British Circus. You wonder how long the fields will remain unbuilt on. Then back into Clacton. Four thirteen-year-old girls had got on the bus at Brooklands. 'Where are we going?' they chanted at the top of their voices. 'Buy *Heat* magazine!' They explained about Essex to two girls who'd come here on holiday. 'Essex is so big, it's got all sorts of counties in it. Ipswich, Colchester, Norfolk.' 'Is it bigger than London?' one of the visitors asked. 'Oh, yes.' 'I didn't know. We're used to country lanes.' 'Nice to meet you. I'll text you my number.'

One of the Jaywick houses is called Peacehaven. A cousinly tribute, I suppose. The two are similar but not identical. Peacehaven itself is where the Greenwich meridian reaches the north edge of English Channel. A stumpy white obelisk, with a green globe on top, marks precisely where 0 degrees longitude plunges over the chalk cliffs of Sussex, due east of Brighton, and swims off south, towards France. I reached the obelisk down a row of red-brick bungalows. The seafront was a strip of grass along the cliff top. A woman was walking her poodle. A photographer from the *Brighton Evening Argus* hovered around the obelisk, taking shots of the chairman of the Peacehaven Residents' Association. The chairman and his wife used to have a caravan near Peacehaven. They liked the place so much that he sold his business in London. About a quarter of the 13,500 people who live in Peacehaven are retired.

Peacehaven is bungalow heaven. This is why it was so detested by Williams-Ellis and his followers. But popular choice is much friendlier to bungalows. Every year, the Royal Institute of British Architects hands out its Stirling Prize. It is named after Britain's best-known and most influential brutalist architect, James Stirling, designer of several unloved buildings in Oxford, Cambridge and the City of London. In 2002, to help publicise the prizegiving, a government quango, the Commission for Architecture and the Built Environment, asked the respected polling firm Mori to check the nation's ideal type of home. Mori chose 1,000 respondents at random locations across England, and showed them photographs of seven different kinds of homes. It asked them where they would most like to live: a bungalow, a traditional village house, a Victorian terrace house, a 1930s semi, a modern semi, a loft apartment and a tower block. To the commission's deep chagrin, the bungalow came top, with 30 per cent of the votes; bungalows are built by builders and developers, not architects. The vast majority of respondents chose one of the suburban options. Only 2 per cent favoured a loft apartment, and no one at all chose a tower block. The endorsement of the suburban way of life could not have been stronger.

Top: Peacehaven's own Mayfield Avenue. Above: Garage art – the call of the wild.

To come to Peacehaven now is to visit yesterday's future. Eric Hobsbawm has written: 'To write about this country

A community that cares. Above left: Peacehaven undertaker. Above right: Doorstep sign announcing 'Two spoilt rotten dogs here' propped against a statuette of a nude.

without also saying something about the West Indies, about Argentina and Australia, is unreal.' The obelisk gave distances not only to Greenwich (48 miles), but also to every corner of the empire: Wellington, Valetta, Rangoon, Gold Coast Town (Accra), Aden and, the furthest-flung, Hong Kong (6,003 miles). The first stone was laid – to mark the 1935 silver jubilee of George V's 'beneficent and illustrious reign' – by Charles Neville, the man who invented Peacehaven. He bought the land from 1915 on. He had previously been a land speculator in Saskatchewan and Australia.

There were bungalows in Britain before this. The first recorded example was built in north Kent in the 1860s. But Peacehaven between the two world wars, with its scattering of cheap homes for heroes, was something new. If any single place was responsible for the first town and country planning legislation, it was Peacehaven. It symbolised how control of the land had slipped through the fingers of the hereditary landlords – who were busy selling up for hard cash. Something had to be done. The odd thing is that Neville, in the photograph I saw in Peacehaven library, looked just like one of the first British politicians to take up the rural protection cause, Stanley Baldwin, three times Conservative Prime Minister between 1923 and 1937, and the dominant figure in interwar politics. In his portrait photo, Neville sat solidly on his chair, cigar in hand, heavy-faced, a watch chain across his waistcoat.

Peacehaven was still almost all bungalows. I stood on the pavement outside No. 180 Arundel Road and saw a long low ripple of rooftops. This was the little man's empire. Neville ran a newspaper competition to choose a name. The judges plumped for New Anzac-on-Sea. But Neville switched the name within six months. Memories of Gallipoli were not the best selling point for his 25 × 100 foot plots, laid out on a simple grid. For the same reason, Ypres Avenue became Downland Avenue, and Marne Avenue became Vernon. The only explicit wartime reminder to survive is more sentimental. Edith and Cavell Avenues commemorate the English nurse executed in Belgium in 1915 by the German army.

Bungalows are an imperial invention. They began as *banggolo*, a Bengali peasant hut. All across British India, public works departments mass-produced a tougher version: cheap, cool and untiring (because stairless). When the captains and the engineers went back to Blighty (Hindi *bilayati*), they took the bungalow style with them. In spite of the continuing derision from the elite, I noticed that in Croydon they were still building them. The Scots – who ran the empire, as soldiers and engineers, almost all the time – seem especially fond of them. I walked around a new housing estate outside the small town of Leven, in Fife. It was named Vettriano Vale, after the painter Jack Vettriano, who was born near here. Bungalows were prominent on the estate. Vettriano's appealingly gaudy, mildly

How new homes are judged by the judgmental: before the flowers grow. An estate in Fife, named after the local-born populist painter.

erotic pictures are dismissed by the cabal of London art critics, and are held in no public gallery outside Fife. (The Kirkcaldy museum and art gallery holds two, one of which was donated by the artist.) But Vettriano paintings, and their poster reproductions, sell and sell. Rather like bungalows.

In Britain, the bungalow soon skittered down the social gradient. But in America, it held onto its Californian charm. Bix Beiderbecke recorded his own cornet tribute with RKO as Wall Street crashed: 'Our little love nest/Beside a stream/Where red, red roses grow/Our bungalow of dreams.' The social history of the bungalow has been chronicled in a fine, scholarly, eccentric book by Anthony D. King. 'In the first half of the twentieth century,' he argued, 'the bungalow was the most revolutionary building type established in Britain.' As the architecture commission's opinion survey demonstrated, the bungalow was, and remains, far more popular than the multi-storey flats which many architects and planners thought were just the job for the working classes. Basil Spence, the Scots-born designer of Coventry Cathedral and Sussex University, designed tall flats to replace the old Gorbals tenements in Glasgow. They have all been demolished. If Spence had gone in for bungalows, the houses would be there still. Very few bungalows-of-dreams have ever been knocked down.

The Rochdale popular singer and film star Gracie Fields (1898–1979), theme tune 'Sally', bought a Peacehaven bungalow for her mother, Sarah Stansfield, and stayed in Peacehaven sometimes in between south coast variety bookings. Peacehaven can lay claim to a pale extension of Brighton's theatrical tradition. The actress Flora Robson made her first public appearance at the Rosemary Tea Rooms in Peacehaven. The great cookery writer Elizabeth David, in her brief career on the stage, played the summer season at the Peacehaven Theatre. The tea rooms and the theatre have been demolished. Peacehaven didn't linger over its past. The future was the thing.

Imperial history rolled on. Bengalis and Kashmiris now live in cotton-town terraces like those the Stansfields abandoned for a bungalow by the sea. Peacehaven, meanwhile, like most of Britain, remained almost entirely white. It has none of the shacks you find at Broadlands in Jaywick Sands, but many of the bungalows are extremely modest. The front gardens I looked into were often neglected, with intermittent hydrangeas and fuchsias, plants you could leave on their own to cope with the gusty wind and salty air. No two houses were exactly the same, though the residents seemed happy to stick to street numbers, rather than names, by contrast with Jaywick. No. 180 Arundel Road was a living fantasy. Two-storeyed, it had windows screened by white curtains and potted plants. A lanky cement greyhound sat by the front door. A tall pole flew an England flag. The doors of the double garage were covered with a huge, photo-realist painting – rather like an overgrown table-coaster – of a dog on the Downs, staring out alertly into the distance. The painted sky was china-blue, the clouds were fluffy, the grass was interspersed with bright red poppies. On the crazy paving in front of the garage, an old Vauxhall Nova.

Peacehaven may have been stopped in its tracks by the planning laws. But it is on the easterly edge of a much more prosperous and effervescent town than Clacton. The writer Keith Waterhouse, a long-time resident, once said that 'Brighton looks like a town that is helping the police with their inquiries'. It fizzes with metropolitan life. As I waited for the bus out to Peacehaven, I noticed that, in homage to the town's rackety past, one of the buses had been named the 'Maria Fitzherbert' after the Prince Regent's unlawful Roman Catholic wife, who lived in Brighton for many years. The pressure to build has not weakened. Developers found a new way round the restrictions when they opened a marina in 1979. It encloses 71 acres of water on the seafront below Brighton's elegant Georgian suburb, Kemptown. And, yes, it has many boats moored, but you can see that the real purpose was to find somewhere new to build quayside homes. The marina's entrance road sweeps down towards a casino, a McDonalds and a multi-storey car park. Peacehaven was a beginning, not an end.

The impetus to get out of city centres, and get on, isn't new. Nor is it weakening. If you define London, rather narrowly, as the area of the Greater London Authority (which means approximately London inside the M25), the population has been rocketing. This rise was widely unpredicted. For many decades, up to about 1990, all plans assumed a population fall. But the upturn was entirely fuelled by new arrivals from abroad, and their children and grandchildren. The numbers of Londoners leaving for greener, suburban or exurban pastures remained as high as it ever was. About 100,000 people left London every year. They settled, mostly, in other parts of southern England. They were voting with their feet and their wallets. It is not only the attraction of more space and more of a garden. There is also the magnetism of better schools, better health care, easier travel. For obvious generational reasons, this flight has so far been mostly white. But as other ethnic groups start their rise up the ladder – Asians and

Chinese especially – they move in the same direction. You could look back at how London's Jewish suburbia grew, in Ilford to the east and Golders Green to the north, after the new arrivals' first settlement in Whitechapel. Gants Hill, in east suburban London, is now home to many aspirant Bangladeshi families who have, in their turn, moved out from Whitechapel.

Time, perhaps, for another touch of history. The Chartists of the early years of the nineteenth century had half a dozen demands for political reform: election by secret ballot, universal (male) suffrage and so forth. Most of these demands were granted over the following half-century or so. But the Chartists also sought a better kind of habitation. They were influenced by Owen's work at New Lanark, or maybe even more so by his book of essays (1813–16), published as *A New View of Society*. In these pages he skimmed over the fact that New Lanark was far from being an exercise in worker control.

The two great leaders of Chartism were Feargus O'Connor and Bronterre O'Brien. They were also great rivals. When O'Connor founded his Chartist Land Company to set up new settlements as a form of workers' self-help, O'Brien derided it for undermining the great aim of land nationalisation. The first settlement was named O'Connorville. It was launched with a march from London to the fields of Hertfordshire – the classic county for habitation experiments, it seems; hence, also, Letchworth, Welwyn and Stevenage. The banner, held up in front of the Chartist march, said: 'Labour's Procession to Labour's own Land, purchased with Labour's own Money.'

At Heronsgate, near Rickmansworth, 103 acres were bought. Up in radical Manchester, O'Connor presided over a ballot for thirty-five smallholdings. He spoke of clear skies and rich soil; of children at school, not in the mill; of vice withering and virtue abounding. On 1 May 1847, the first tenants moved in. Ten years later, the bankrupt estate was auctioned off. An experiment was over. The way forward, it turned out, was the building society movement, also nurtured by northern working men. The Halifax became the biggest of these.

I was kindly shown a reprint of a Chartist poster by the people who now live in the solid brick schoolhouse O'Connor built. I was touched to see that plot No. 31 (4 acres) was taken by James Greenwood, from Hebden Bridge. Greenwood was the first to sell off his allocation. O'Connor's *Northern Star* newspaper carried angry correspondence. I like to think it was sheer Yorkshire shrewdness. The newfangled name, O'Connorville, was soon ditched, and long

The Chartists, in 1847, built homes for aspirant working families. This house in Charterville, Hertfordshire (since renamed Heronsgate) carries the logo of the People's Charter on its gable end.

forgotten. But on the 150th anniversary, in 1997, the Heronsgate Association celebrated O'Connorville with a barbecue (roast pork and stovepipe hats). An old Wesleyan chapel acquired a fine blue plaque: 'In proud memory of O'Connorville' and of 'Feargus O'Connor MP. Chartist, Idealist and Social Reformer.'

To get there, I'd turned off the M25 at exit 17, and plunged into gentle countryside. The charms of exurban life. In half a mile I was among some discordantly gritty-sounding addresses: Nottingham, Stockport, Bradford and Halifax Roads. All were named after the towns where the early supporters came from. O'Connor made the roads only 9 feet wide; more like lanes. Hawthorn and laurel overhung them. Houses in Heronsgate were much sought after, I was told. It is a private Arcadian world, but no longer an Arcadia for all. The smallholdings, never less than 2 acres, had become huge gardens with luxuriant trees, swimming pools, double or triple garages (some of them as big as O'Connor's original cottages). A Mercedes for him, for example, and a Hyundai hatchback for her. I looked out over fields of meadowsweet, or into paddocks. A man cycled by, exercising two liver-coloured Weimaraners.

The houses had been rebuilt and enlarged. But enwrapped within many of them, I could see evidence of how it all began: a modest but elegant two-storey semi, in classical style. Each of these gable ends bore O'Connor's little device: a logo of the People's Charter, partly unscrolled, like a sacred text. As a businessman, O'Connor failed. No great disgrace in that. Sidney and Beatrice Webb, chroniclers of socialism in action, noted sourly, but rightly, that the question of how to manage things was the big stumbling block for all workers' control organisations: who should have the final say? But O'Connor planned better than he is given credit for. A semi, in something as much like countryside as possible, has become an enduring English ideal. Or if not a semi, a bungalow.

This ideal has withstood all the eco-campaigners' and New Urbanists' arguments that the only correct preference is a close-knit street house or a town flat. This is not to argue against the environmentalist desire to make new houses as energy-efficient as possible. Nor against wish of the New Urbanist movement – whose anti-Corbusian programme was launched in 1996 – to cherish the tradition, within inner cities, of building in streets. But the planner Michael Hebbert, though a sympathiser with the New Urbanism, observes that the 'attempt to invent workable pattern-languages for the cores, middle zones, suburbs and outer parts of compact cities is extraordinarily heroic'. (This sounds a bit like Sir Humphrey, in *Yes Minister*, telling the twitchy minister how 'very brave' his latest proposal is.) Hebbert reports that sceptics have apparently compared the New Urbanism to 'the quixotic undertaking of Pierre Menard, the Borges character who immerses himself in the study of Spanish, history and Catholicism in the hope of becoming able to rewrite Don Quixote word for word'. Energy-efficient houses can be achieved through tight building regulations. And there should always be a gentle bias towards preserving the streets: they are a city's memory bank. Neither should be achieved at the cost of preventing people living the life they wish to have.

In his Chartist settlement, O'Connor's villas, with their fitted book-shelves, surprised contemporaries: they were of 'tradesman' rather than 'working man' standard. The pity is that almost all subsequent council and social housing slid back into building dwellings which were immediately recognisable, even to the casual eye, as housing for the poor. In 1847, a celebratory verse enthused:

> Has Freedom whispered in his wistful ear,
> 'Courage, poor slave! Deliverance is near'?
> Oh, she has breathed a summons sweeter still.
> 'Come, take your garden at O'Connorville.'

There are sixty houses now in these green lanes. 'It's the sort of place you only leave in a box,' a man said as he swept up in front of the church. Even then, you could come back. Your ashes could be scattered in the little garden behind the church. In the chancel I found a brass to Frederick Felkin, born in Nottingham in 1834, died 1903. He must have been one of the handful of settlers who stayed on. The present citizens of O'Connorville were not amused when the local Labour Party tried to use the church porch, one election year, as a nomination platform. O'Connor would have sympathised with the residents. 'My plan has no more to do with socialism,' he wrote, 'than it has to do with a comet.'

Like many reformers, O'Connor was better at giving instructions than at following them. He lived at Hope Cottage (re-christened as Hope Lodge, with resident poodle), where he fathered two sons by a local woman, but didn't marry her. He insisted that O'Connorville should be dry, but he himself died of drink. Just outside the settlement limits, I found a pub called The Land of Liberty, Peace and Plenty. Its array of real ale included Umpire's Best, from the Mighty Oak Brewery in Essex, Conservation Bitter, from the Red Squirrel Brewery, 25 miles away, and Shepherd Neame's Spitfire Bitter, which duly made donations to the RAF Benevolent Fund. The Land of Liberty had been chosen for an award by Camra (the Campaign for Real Ale), Britain's most successful consumer protest group. A Camra table mat chirruped: 'A Pub is for Life, Not Just for Christmas.' The front of the pub sign showed O'Connor speaking in favour of voting by ballot. The reverse showed King John signing the Magna Carta. O'Connorville was a good place to muse about freedom, and what it should amount to.

5. STRIVING AND RELAXING

I had a vision of one kind of future as I sat and watched the shoppers at 'Bicester Village': pleasant, calm, suburban, safe. The very nicest middling experience. The shoppers walked along the perfect paving between white wooden planters, filled with fuchsias. They cruised the low, white, weather-boarded shops. Everyone was very trim. I saw only one beer belly and hardly any serious tattoos. Hair was newly washed, often newly cut. Jeans and trousers were spotlessly dry-cleaned. (Hardly any women wore skirts.) There weren't many children. Most hands held a shopping bag. I was tempted into the pop-psychology of couples, from their bags. What, exactly, was the distinction between a Versace-Jaeger couple and a Hobbs-Timberland couple?

Bicester Village is a village in a new, Middle England sense. It goes one step beyond the standard, semi-deserted, second-home village. No one at all lives in it. It is an 'outlet village' of the kind which has been spreading nation-wide. Cheshire Oaks is a prosperous version on the Wirral: a peninsula which is still Cheshire at heart, even though the administrative boundary-drawers have re-assigned it to Merseyside. To reach Bicester Village I took exit 9 off the M40, just north of Oxford. The town of Bicester isn't much larger than a village itself, but Bicester Village is on its outskirts, just beyond a huge Tesco. It looked like a slice of New England – or, conceivably, Suffolk – transplanted to the English Midlands. Steeply pitched roofs rose above the weather-boarding. In the middle was what looked like the dark-green turret of a town hall, with a gilt clock-face; in fact, it was the Polo Ralph Lauren store. The village had a single high street, which at one end had yet more building work going ahead for new shops. All were called boutiques. In this sort-of mall, the usual department store 'anchors' – John Lewis, Boots, Debenhams, Marks & Spencer – got no look-in. There was no Primark. If you were hungry, Starbucks and Prêt à Manger were here, but they were counterbalanced by Carluccio and Villandry.

It was an optical-illusion village. Here solely to give street space to clothes shops selling superior discount goods: ends of lines, and some seconds. I suspect that New Urbanists would disapprove, in spite of the street's oblique, even

Opposite: Taking the weight off your feet on the 'high street' at Bicester Village, Oxfordshire, an optical-illusion hamlet, devoted to selling clothes.

playful, homage to their principles. Bicester Village was surrounded by parking lots. On my first visit, in order to capture the flavour, I had walked down the first row of cars I came to: very few brand-new, but none very old, either: Audis, Saabs, BMWs. Prosperous, but not rich. As I stood with my notebook that day, a security man materialised and asked me bluntly what I was doing. Bicester Village was as full of closed-circuit TV scanners as any big-bang shopping mall, or the pedestrianised zone of any 'real' town, or the movie mock-suburbia of *The Truman Show* (which is set in a real New Urbanist model village, Seaside, Florida). In the office, once I'd explained myself, I was put through on the phone to the boss, who was in his London headquarters. Scott Malkin said he saw Bicester Village as 'in the arena of running a department store' (open-air version). Here were Ozwald Boateng, Gieves & Hawkes, Aquascutum, Nicole Farhi, Paul Smith; but also the shops you might find on any city main street: French Connection, Monsoon, Whistles, Jigsaw. Educationists fret about Britain's high rate of illiteracy; but more and more of the future seems to turn on having the right label. A short-cut to showing you're in the middle of the middle.

The cheaper shops were still not very cheap. The point was partly to put off mass shoppers. The company didn't want too many people drifting in from the Tesco. Bicester Village is, handily, halfway between London and Birmingham, but it is also handy for tourism: Stratford-on-Avon, Blenheim Palace, the Cotswolds (meaning the knick-knack shops and eateries of Broadway, Stow-on-the-Wold, Chipping Camden). After the village opened, in 1995, shoppers mainly came either through word of mouth, I was told, or through travel firms. By my last visit, there were more than three million visitors a year, about 65 per cent of them tourists, roughly half and half British and overseas. The stage-set high street isn't for regular shoppers, but for people who might stop in on their way somewhere else. It was shopping as a form of entertainment.

In the village information office they were making a special thing of Flora Thompson. Her moving memoir of agricultural poverty is set, 100 years back, in this same north Oxfordshire countryside. A guidebook, *The World of Flora Thompson Revisited*, told you how to see where she'd lived, once you'd checked out the jeans and jumpers. As recorded in *Lark Rise to Candleford*, her world was hedged about by class. Bicester Village was purveying classiness – which is different. Writing in the *International Herald Tribune*, the fashion editor

Suzy Menkes suggested that 'Bicester Village is selling a modern dream: that nice middle class people with limited incomes can buy nice things from nice salespeople in nice surroundings. Sales hopping need not be grubby and grabby.' It was, she wrote, 'the lure of a bargain with a touch of class'.

The model (and part of the finance) for Bicester Village was American. But it was Anglophile American, like the novels of Henry James. The decor in the Ralph Lauren shop included battered suitcases, which were meant to exude a smell of Old Money, and even of the Old Country. I suppose that is also why the Ralph Lauren shops' founder changed his surname from Lifschitz. In this fantasy village in the middle of Oxfordshire, the goods embodied class you could buy. The new Oxford, not of dreaming spires, but of dreamy shelves. 'I have a Vision of The Future, chum,' Betjeman wrote. His poem 'The Planster's Vision' mocked not only the postwar planners but also the prole-cult poets of the 1930s. Bicester Village embodied another cult, and another future. Oxford itself, in its central streets, served by the park-and-ride buses (which draw more and more people in from surrounding small towns and villages), now encapsulates the same passion for retail.

On this journey, I was in a Tolkien-like quest for Middle England, which I'd argue is little more than a grand phrase for suburbia. Bicester Village was a kind of pilgrimage site. It struck me as the twenty-first-century version of that medieval chain of towns on the route to Santiago de Compostela, each of them trying to offer the very best relics and the cosiest inns. Today Chaucer's Canterbury pilgrims would drink less, and buy more.

Driving on towards Stratford-on-Avon, I came to the Rollright Stones. A helpful young man was today's warden, sitting under a blue canvas awning at the sort of table at which they sell tickets at a church fête. The last time I'd visited, a middle aged man looked out at the stones from his little wooden hut, with the weariness of wardens the world over. A trust had been set up to try to defend these once-obscure megalithic remains, now thought by some to

The very nicest suburban experience at Bicester Village: pleasant, calm, safe.

be magical. Passionate pilgrims of the non-retail kind – paganists, satanists, pantheists, and the merely curious like me – had threatened to overwhelm them with their hugs, kisses and sheer weight of feet. The young man told me that seventy visitors a day was normal. Sometimes, on a Sunday, there would be 400, many of them cyclists. This time there was no hut. It had been burned down. A car in the lay-by had a rear-window sticker: 'Wiccans are spell-binding people.' Maybe they also play with fire.

Was this the other side of suburban Middle England, I asked myself. Many of the components were here: a rural dream, a hint of do-it-yourself, a reliance on voluntary work, a scarcely hidden eccentricity. The trust's brochures and website mentioned ley-lines, witchcraft, druidism and aliens. You could book the space inside the stones for Wiccan hand-fasting and blessings. To my eye there was little magic left, but it might be different at sunrise or sunset.

Before the arson of the hut, the big trouble had been paint vandalism. All the stones were sprayed. The site manager had to try to work out how to get it off without destroying the lichen. On the wall of the old hut I remembered a bleached-out CCTV photo of a young man suspected of paint-daubing: £1,000 reward. Why do it? 'People are people,' the then warden said. 'Some have a grudge, or think they can change the world. Him, perhaps, he'd had a row with his girlfriend the night before, and she was a pagan. Who knows?'

Was I getting close to the suburban grail? Middle England goes to great lengths to feel safe. Bicester Village is, among other things, a cathedral of safeness. Within this cathedral, the religion of niceness is worshipped. (But isn't niceness preferable to nastiness?) Like the wardens of the stones, Middle England often uses crime as a social yardstick. Three criminologists, Evi Girling, Ian Loader and Richard Sparks, wrote one of the rare academic studies with 'Middle England' in the title. Their *Crime and Social Change in Middle England* investigated social attitudes in Macclesfield in Cheshire, 'this unremarkable, relatively untroubled, moderately prosperous English town'. An exurb of Manchester, it was the home of Brian Redhead, former editor of the *Manchester Evening News* and long-time cheery presenter of BBC Radio 4's *Today* programme. Redhead made Macclesfield one of the trademarks of his broadcasting personality.

The three academics wondered what 'people may be saying when they speak about crime'. Here, and in most parts of Britain, they decided, people are not truly fretting about the detailed police statistics. In reality, crime-talk – now as common as talk about parking or the weather – touches on questions 'to do with justice and welfare, inclusion and exclusion, the respective roles of citizen and state'. The 'anxieties and aspirations' related to 'order, civility and respectability': the suburbanist creed. Socially, the researchers concluded, the people they studied often see themselves as 'spectators watching dramas in which they play little part'. Publishing in 2000, before any widely feared Islamist terror threat in Britain, the authors decided that: 'The antique dilemma between liberty and security arises afresh each time and in each place we encounter it.' Suburb dwellers reckon they have squared that circle, gaining both liberty and security, by comparison with the central city. Crime isn't only a question of psychology. The Rollright Stones had in fact been damaged.

'Middle England' has become a political cliché as a blanket alternative to 'suburbia'. It crops up with unfailing regularity in reports and commentaries. Nor is it just party politics. Explaining the ratings success of her BBC TV comedy show, *Goodness Gracious Me*, about an argumentative Indian family, the actress Meera Syal said: 'The excitement was: hang on a minute, this isn't just Asians that are listening to it. This is Middle England.' When Prince Charles married Camilla Parker-Bowles, the *Daily Telegraph* hired four poets to write epithalamia. They described one of them, Pam Ayres, as 'comic poet/poetess to Middle England'. Her poem, in full, was:

> My mother said, 'Say *nothing*,
> If you can't say something nice.'
> So from my poem you can see
> I'm taking her advice.

If suburban Middle England is a comfort blanket for the right, it is a hair shirt for the left. Many leftists follow, unknowingly, in the footsteps of Clough Williams-Ellis. For them, the term seems have become a mere yah-boo scatter-gun insult (as 'bourgeois' once was, and 'fascist' still is), aimed at anything that is disliked. If I were asked to pin down Middle England's habitat, I would point to all the avenues, closes and crescents of suburbia, and the no-through-road cul-de-sacs invented by Raymond Unwin at Letchworth, and endlessly imitated. Some have their doubts. Peter Hall, author of *Cities of Tomorrow* and *Cities in Civilisation*, suggests that 'Middle England doesn't exist in Euclidean space but in the mind'. R.E. Pahl disagrees. He has been researching theories of relative deprivation (poverty defined not as destitution, but as falling behind), of which the corollary is how to keep up with the Joneses or the Shahs. To Pahl, Middle England does mean 'estate culture and how you grade estates: all comparing cars and reading the *Daily Mail*. You can reach there by any means, perhaps you left school at fourteen, but it's all evened out on that estate.' In many people's minds, Pahl thinks, such social gradings have largely overtaken the language of class: the new divide is between 'people like us' and the rest (though Pahl himself favours a tripartite analytical division, into senior salariat, middle mass and underclass).

Mockery of Middle England is impossible to separate out from the usual sneers against suburbia. In the heyday of Attlee's 1945–51 government, the Education Minister was a former leftist firebrand called Ellen Wilkinson. She had once led the famous Jarrow hunger march to London. In 1947, referring to the newly founded forerunner of Radio 3, she told a lecture audience that she wanted Britain to be a Third Programme nation. Whatever they may think in private, politicians can seldom publicly display such metropolitan haughtiness. They are obliged to continue their pursuit of the semi-attached voters, living in the new estates of the realm, who are more likely to listen to Radios 1, 2 and 4, or Classic FM. When Tony Blair had his great electoral triumph, in 1997, ending eighteen years of Conservative government, a little cartoonish figure was set up to represent the elusive but crucial Middle England. This was 'Mondeo man', defined by his Ford family car; likeliest names, Gary or Barry; emblematic home county, Thatcherite Essex.

Many, including Pahl, define Middle England by its reading matter: the *Daily Mail* or the *Mail on Sunday*. Totting up the respondents to its opinion surveys, Mori found that, among national daily papers, the readership of the *Daily Mail* came closest to the male–female population divide (47 and 53 per cent, against the national 49 and 51 per cent). By the same reckoning, the *Guardian* had more men, proportionately; its readership also tended to be younger. The two

Is the new social divide between 'People Like Us' (PLU) and the rest? Brookmans Park, Hertfordshire, is up the road, in every sense, from unglamorous Potters Bar.

newspapers are like sparring partners, fighting over the soul of Middle England (which the *Mail*, for variety's sake, sometimes re-dubs 'MidEngland'). Each of these papers has the great merit of a clear ethic – though this doesn't mean that everything in the paper follows a predictable line. The liberal-minded were taken by surprise when the *Mail* courageously named the presumed killers of young Stephen Lawrence, after his racist murder in 1993.

The centre-left *Guardian* is obsessed by its centre-right rival. Checking back eight years, I found that the newspaper had carried almost 16,000 mentions of the *Daily Mail*, plus another 8,000 for the *Mail on Sunday*. This seemed to be shorthand for 'people *not* like us' (PNLU?). The confrontations over issues, between the *Guardian* and the *Mail*, often turn on separating 'popular' from 'populist'. The awkward truth is that what is popular, even populist, is not always wrong. The pros and cons of suburbia illustrate this very clearly. In 1956, a prominent Labour revisionist, Anthony Crosland, wrote an iconoclastic polemic *The Future of Socialism*, which became the gospel for those in the party who wanted to edge away from the old Marxist shibboleths. In his onslaught, Crosland attacked Lord Beaverbrook's *Daily Express* – then a flourishing mid-market paper, roughly the equivalent of today's *Daily Mail* – for advocating more privately owned family houses and gardens, instead of bright new council inner-city flats. The mid-market *Express* foresaw future preferences better than the more intellectual Crosland.

The *Daily Mail*'s Ideal Home show, dating from 1908, is Middle England come to town: suburbia invades Earl's Court. The exhibition organisers' breakdowns show two thirds of the visitors to be women, half aged twenty-four to forty-four and 82 per cent 'middle class' (social groups, A, B and C1, in marketing jargon). When I went along, I found that the press office had pinned up clippings from such papers as the *Western and Somerset Mercury*, the *Brackley and Towcester Advertiser* and *Jewish News*. I went through the Earl's Court turnstiles among many mother-and-daughter couples. The mothers' jeans were embroidered; the daughters dressed more casually.

The theme that year was the Mediterranean. The first thing I saw was the Mediterranean House. It was all purple, black and pink. In the living room were black, hand-dyed carpets, black and purple walls, black and purple wing-chairs with brass studs; even the cocktail glasses had purple-tinted stems. In the bedroom the carpet was hand-dyed 'outrageous magenta-pink'; the tables were black metal. 'Think Coco Chanel and Pierre Cardin', the designers said. 'Think *Hello* magazine. Think drama to the power of ten with a style factor of a thousand.' Or you could think 'Middle England gone gaudy'. And why not?

I passed a poster that asked: 'Is Croatia the new Marbella?' Despite this, a salesman tried to tempt me with a house on the 'Costa Blanca,' south of Alicante. He was lightly but evenly tanned, his hair gently grizzled, his eye contact unswerving. He told me he'd served twenty-three years in the army, then went into the police. But he and his wife weren't seeing enough of each other. 'So we released the equity on our Welwyn Garden City house, moved to Spain, and everything took off.' (I don't think he would say the same thing now.) He gave me a sales pack, with a yellow plastic Spanish fan, taped with user instructions: how to display it to say 'I love you,' or, failing that, 'I remember you'.

A team of young women were decorating a house, in a London radio competition. The winner would get £2,000. Each of them had chosen a life motto: 'Smile and the world smiles with you' (Helen); 'Just get on with it' (Tracey); 'Seize the day' (Lori). Helen stated that her 'worst job' was 'delivering telephone directories with my mum'. Gay's 'proudest achievement' was contriving, as a single mother, to work, run a home, be mother to three children, 'and managing to remain sane (just)'.

The show's exhibits were a complex suburban mixture of striving and relaxing. The London School of Investment said: 'Get Educated! Get Active! Take Control!' Inspire Decor sold mottoes to put up on your walls: a still of Audrey Hepburn from *Breakfast at Tiffany's*, with the quote, 'I never thought that I'd land in pictures with a face like mine'. But everywhere also tempted you to relax – after or before striving. Doze on your 'African Shades' reed-thatched garden seat. Join the queue for the free makeover by the London College of Beauty Therapy; surrounded by the odour of nail polish, a harpist played; wedding bookings were welcomed. Patent massage chairs with little automatic pommels, patent massage beds with multiple positions: everything to help ease neck pain, back pain, leg pain, all the pains of Middle England life. The cat could have a relaxing time, too, in a suede-lined cat-sleeper called Winks. I wasn't sure what spray-on nylon was about. You should always ask. 'It's for a hot day,' the saleswoman said. 'You don't need to keep pulling your tights up. It won't ladder. You can wear it with sandals.' Then a pause. 'It's for those who don't have perfect legs, to be honest.' I thought this counted as striving, not relaxing.

As a political idea, Middle England was an import from America, where it is undoubtedly a real place, both geographically and socially. *Time* magazine always has an award for man or woman of the year. On 5 January 1970, it honoured both sexes: Man and Woman of the Year were 'The Middle Americans', otherwise known to political history as the Silent Majority. Student rioting on 1960s American campuses resulted, not in revolution, but in the 1968 election of Richard Nixon as president. The Middle Americans, *Time* reported, 'in the bumper sticker dialogue of the freeways', answered 'Make Love Not War' with 'Honor America'. 'In Minneapolis they elected a police detective to be mayor . . . By their silent but newly felt presence, they influenced the mood of government and the course of legislation.' As always, Britain tagged along. In 2002, Middlesburgh elected a former detective superintendent as mayor. In

A suburban, but rarely achieved, ideal. Looking out from Ilkley towards the famous moor.

London's 2008 mayoral race, a former assistant commissioner of police tried to pull off the same trick (but failed).

Sam Francis was a columnist on the hard-right *Middle American News* for many years until his death in 2005. In one essay he wrote: 'Middle American radicals are essentially middle-income, white, often ethnic [but not black], voters who see themselves as an exploited and dispossessed group, excluded from meaningful political participation, threatened by the tax and trade policies of the government, victimised by its tolerance of crime, immigration and social deviance, and ignored or ridiculed by the major cultural institutions of the media and education.' Yet, he argued, they were the 'core population group providing America its essential history, culture and identity'. Francis gave his intellectual influences as James Burnham, Machiavelli and Pareto, all analysts of elites. He managed to get himself expelled from the ultra-conservative John Birch Society. The 'drive for "diversity",' he said, 'was just rationalisation by US elites to cloak demand for cheap labour'. In Britain, the attack on 'vibrant multiculturalism' made the same point.

I suspect that Sam Francis was not a nice man to know. But he certainly didn't pussyfoot. Part of his identification of Middle-ism fitted the English phenomenon. For example, white flight – and some brown flight – from English cities has been little discussed, but it exists. Stratford-upon-Avon could be one candidate town for the capital of Middle England. When I reached there on my quest, I saw scarcely a non-white face in the street. At the Royal Shakespeare Company's Swan Theatre, I watched a deeply obscure Elizabethan play, *Sir Thomas More*. The 'colour-blind' – that is, highly colour-conscious – casting meant that there were more black actors on stage than visibly ethnic-minority members in the suburbanite audience. Curiously, the first act of the play – written by a handful of hacks, apart from a single speech by Shakespeare – was largely about Londoners rioting against foreigners, which then meant French, Dutch and Lombards. 'It is hard when Englishmen's patience must be thus jetted [encroached] on by strangers,' the chief rioter says, 'and they dare not revenge their own wrongs.'

Stratford-on-Avon was swelling out in all directions. It was handy for escapees from commuter-distance Birmingham or Coventry. New flats overlooked the racecourse. On the Banbury Road the sales-flags of three big developers, Bryant, Kier and Persimmon, fluttered bravely over a large new red-brick estate.

Admittedly, Middle England may be a clutch of pieces in a social jigsaw, rather than one continuous place. (But that is also true of suburbia.) It seems like a jigsaw if you look at Mosaic UK, a census-based analysis developed by the spatial analyst Richard Webber for the Nottingham-based company Experian. Mosaic UK breaks the country down by postcode (fourteen or fifteen households each) and, for every postcode, weaves together census material, credit ratings, family expenditure, car ownership and other special surveys. All households were then allocated to one of sixty-one types, which were combined into eleven larger groups. These groups included Happy Families (Darren and Joan, 10.76 per cent of UK households), Suburban Comfort (Geoffrey and Valerie, 15.10 per cent), Welfare Borderline (Joseph and Agnes, 6.43 per cent), Blue Collar Enterprise (Dean and Mandy, 11.01 per cent) and Grey Perspectives (Edgar and Constance, 7.88 per cent). Within Suburban Comfort, the six sub-types included Small Time Business and Sprawling Subtopia. Somewhere between these two, Richard Webber told me, he would expect to find emblematic Middle England (though both types, together, add up to only 6.01 per cent of UK households). They flourish notably, he suggested, in small towns like Havant, outside Portsmouth, or Gillingham, in north Kent; or, on a larger scale, in Milton Keynes. 'Places where people have the choice of lots of jobs. They may not have much education; they may drive white vans. But they are optimists; they borrow money [or used to]; they have never belonged to unions.'

Though it is now an independent company, Experian began as a subsidiary of the giant retailer GUS Ltd, which also at that time owned the Argos stores and ran the country's largest home catalogue. Experian's core business is as a credit ratings checker. Mosaic UK was intended to be used by the retail trade. If you wanted to revamp a pub, was it in the right district for an upmarket design, or should it evoke *Coronation Street*'s Rover's Return? But the Labour and Conservative parties both signed up. After your focus groups had helped to decide key issues, which streets within swing constituencies should you target? The police and other parts of the public sector also began to use Mosaic. It is fascinating to trawl through. You could say that, often, it is a substitute for a long-lost personal knowledge of localities.

Richard Webber had warned me: 'There are no average neighbourhoods any more.' Driving south from Stratford, I passed through small towns and villages with new estates on the outskirts. Mothers were bringing their four-year-olds back from nursery school. The Horseshoe Inn advertised Cypriot Night and Mexican Night. The Self-Drive Hire Centre, in open countryside, offered a Drive-In Barber's and a Nail Bar as extras. Along the road I avoided dead pheasants and live squirrels. I turned off towards Chipping Norton, the very model of a quiet Cotswolds town, and went for a pee at the gents underneath the grand classical town hall, now mostly used for dances and parties. The lavatories were disgusting. The West Oxfordshire district council had put up a public service noticeboard: 'The toilet was last cleaned at _____. Your cleaner's name is _____.' In black ink someone had scribbled in the first blank space 'Christmas', and in the second 'Lazy Cunt'. Very reasonable comments in the circumstances.

Seven motorbikes were parked outside the coffee shop opposite: Kawasaki, Royal Enfield, Norton. It was like a conclave of special delivery couriers. Inside, the day-outing riders were politely eating cookies and almond slices. None of them would see forty again, and some were well past fifty. I picked up the *Chipping Norton News*. 'In our near-classless town,' one article began, jokily, 'one person looks down on everyone else'; it was the crane driver at a big building site. Under the headline, 'Robbery in Town', I found that a retired policeman now made a hobby of reminiscing to groups like the Chipping Norton Rotary Club about the 1963 Great Train Robbery in nearby Buckinghamshire. This was a crime so far in the past as to be comforting, almost picturesque. You could relax.

So is the only true Middle England a suburban pick'n'mix? In 2004, in *Class, Self and Culture*, a London University sociologist Beverley Skeggs announced the arrival of 'identity politics' and the 'choosing, self-managing individual'. People, she argued, now needed to 'make one's life a work of art', and women were the predominant makers of taste. She interpreted the omnipresent junk term, 'lifestyle', as a hunt for cultural 'prostheses': add-ons that redefine who you are. The only snag in Skeggs's argument is that the traditional constraints of most sociology are true. You are sure you are making your own personal choice, but you end up in the same (or similar) suburb, buying the same clothes from the same shop, having the same worries about the children's school, after giving them names which caused you both such anguished debate – only to find that half the nursery school class are named the same. The same sweets are always the favourites in your local Odeon's much-in-the-film pick'n'mix display.

In north Oxfordshire, where Flora Thompson was born into a life of respectable poverty in 1876, there was a place for everything, and for everyone. As I drove back towards Bicester (which was one of Flora Thompson's nearest market towns), other cars started to crowd around me, making their way to the retail village. This was the new suburban Middle England economy in action. At the village there were only five cycles in the bike park. Next to them was a large white coach. Once, the city of Coventry, picking itself up after the wartime blitz, prided itself on building the first all-pedestrian shopping plaza in Europe. Fashion skitters on. The tour coach was from the University of Coventry. The pull of Bicester Village's version of classiness was irresistible.

Like suburbia itself, 'Middle England', as a phrase, gets tangled up with middlebrow, middle market and middle class. It is something you subjectively *believe* you confect for yourself – whether, objectively, you do or not. Bicester Village would never offer pick 'n' mix. But it offers its own version of this. It is a myth of fragrance. No one lives here. But then no one lives at the Rollright Stones or at Disney World, Orlando (cheap flights weekly). To spur the peasantry into rebellion, the unruly priest John Ball had his own dream: 'When Adam delved and Eve span/Who was then the gentleman?' The Middle England of suburbia dreams differently; but it, too, rocks the old, established order, of country versus city, and of 'People Like Us' versus 'People Like Them'.

Cinema architecture reached a high point in suburbia. This page: Gaumont, chinoiserie style (1929), Southall, west London, became a shopping hall (as here); now it is a Bollywood cinema, the Himalaya. Opposite, top left: Grosvenor cinema (1936), Rayners Lane, north-west London (deepest Metroland), became a bar, then a Zoroastrian religious centre. Top right: The Point, Milton Keynes (1985, as built), Britain's first multiplex. Below: Film Works multiplex (2001), Millennium Village, Greenwich, south-east London.

6. YES, BUT WHAT USE IS IT?

Suburbia is a prime example of what David Edgerton has called The Shock of the Old. In his book of that name, subtitled *Technology and Global History since 1900*, Edgerton didn't write about house building at any great length. But he very well could have. His thesis was doubly heretical since he was a professor at Imperial College, London, the heartland of the technocracy. He was attacking the recurrent obsession with the supposed wonders of the future. This is an ailment that architects seem especially vulnerable to. Suburbs, being usually non-architect designed, seem to last forever. Inner city structures, some 'iconic', some not, are more often architect-designed, and seem more vulnerable to demolition. In London alone, 384 tower blocks were built between 1964 and 1971. Many would be abandoned within twenty years. Edgerton writes:

> When we are told about technology from on high, we are made to think that about novelty and the future . . . There are new things under the sun, and the world is indeed changing radically, but this way of thinking is not among them. . . . Reheated futurism has held its appeal long after it was declared obsolete. . . . By thinking about technology-in-use, a radically different picture of technology, and indeed of invention and innovation, becomes possible.

The crucial words are: 'in use'. In other words: how are things in practice, not on the drawing board? What works, as opposed to what is 'at the cutting edge'. In his iconoclastic book, *How Buildings Learn*, Stewart Brand went round and photographed much-lauded modern buildings and showed how they had, or had not, stood up to wear and tear, and how they had been re-shaped, even re-built, by the people who actually lived or worked in them. Many architects were deeply offended. All architecture magazines continue to run photographs of an architect's work in the glossy first-morning shoot. More often first evening, in fact, because most contemporary buildings – even those that purport to be sustainable – look best in the dusk with all their interior lights ablaze. (I have sometimes wondered if 'sustainable' will end up as simply a style, like Modernist, Art Nouveau or

Opposite: The white (suburban) roses of Yorkshire.

Perpendicular. An award-winning 'eco home' in the West Country was advertised for sale, which had a timber frame donated by a local farmer and insulation shorn from local sheep. But it had parking for four cars.)

In the case of some domestic inventions, the question of how – if at all – they work, may not matter much. David Edgerton quotes the findings of a survey by an insurance company, which suggested that there were £3.2 billion-worth of unused goods in British homes. They were mostly in the furthest recesses of the kitchen, or parked on a dusty shelf in the garage. The list was headed by sandwich toasters, electric knives, soda streams (for making fizzy drinks), foot spas and ice cream makers. There were estimated to be 3.4 million unused fondue sets. Most of these items are probably the misjudged gifts, or misplaced hopes, of suburbia. All part of the attempt to be slightly different from, or in advance of, the neighbours. But at least the house itself has not been discarded.

When the art directors of the future wish to deck out a cinema or TV image of the early twenty-first-century home, they will no doubt set out a selection of these useless objects in some very visible place. Life, as Edgerton points out, is not like that. Why the settings of costume dramas look so strange is because, faced with a drama set in 1995, or 1945, or 1895, the researchers will hunt out every possible item that relates to that exact date: house, furniture, wallpaper, cutlery, hats, coats, dresses. But people would live then as they live now, in a lifestyle smorgasbord of items from the distant past, the recent past and the present: the second-hand house, the sofa from Aunt Maud, the cutlery from the wedding present list, topped up by the latest dresses, as stocked by the local high street or retail park shops. And at every stage, things will sometimes have been discarded, but very often stuck away somewhere, in a sentimental tribute to guilt or nostalgia. But for that, how would bric-a-brac dealers ever make a living?

The bank holiday destination of choice for suburbia is the nearest IKEA store. The blue and yellow delivery vans all carry the slogan 'Home is the Most Important Place'. Edgerton suggests that Ingvar Kamprad, of IKEA, should be applauded at business seminars at least as enthusiastically as Bill Gates of Microsoft. Kamprad made his money from mass-producing wooden furniture: a invention which goes back to the nineteenth-century discovery that you could steam-press beech timber into bentwood chairs. The early Modernists held up the bentwood chair as one herald of a technological future: a forebear of the house as 'a machine for living in'. But they didn't quite mean a future of IKEA flat-packs crammed into the Sunday-morning hatchback on the way to No. 23 Acacia Avenue.

Edgerton cites Bruno Latour's book *Nous n'avons jamais été modernes* ('We Have Never Been Modern'). The French sociologist argued that 'modern time . . . has never existed'. Edgerton backs him up with many entertaining statistics. Most soberly: Hitler's Wehrmacht used more horses to get to Moscow than Napoleon's Grande Armée, and took longer. More cheerfully: globally since the late 1960s, many more bicycles have been produced each year than cars. The production of books continues to increase. Ageing (and even dead) 1960s rock stars still generate huge ticket sales. The twenty-first-century child is brought up with Disney films seen by their grandparents when they were children. Now that everything can so easily be recorded and reproduced, the past never goes away. Edgerton concludes that 'The historical study of things in use, and the uses of things, matters'. Not just 'the famous spectacular technologies but the low and ubiquitous ones'.

Walking round suburbia will seldom, if ever, give you the shock of the new. It may shock you, however, with the uses to which the old can be put. Take the Levittowns, which captivated the sociologist H.J. Gans. They were built by William J. Levitt's firm of developers to meet the American postwar demand for suburban houses (a yearning stoked up, from 1956, by the interstate highways programme), and to meet that demand cheap. Levitt's techniques were learnt from war contracts for fast, low-cost housing at military bases. The Levittowns were targeted primarily at war veterans and their discharge gratuities. Levitt's *Guardian* obituary, in 1994, noted that the first Levittown was set down in a Long Island potato field, 10 miles outside the New York city boundary, in 1947. There were 17,000 near-identical homes, all on lots of 60 × 100 feet. Each house had its picture window for its 12 × 16 foot living room, two bedrooms, a kitchen, a bathroom and an attic, which could be fitted out as two more bedrooms. Every house came fitted with a cooker, a fridge, a washing machine and a television set. Ex-servicemen could move in with no down payment; non-veterans had to put 5 per cent down; or the homes could be rented, with an option to buy. Everything was mass-produced, with the construction of each house broken down into twenty-six semi-skilled stages, each with its own crew. At the peak, Levitt's teams could turn out thirty-seven new houses a day.

Other Levittowns quickly followed, in Pennsylvania first, and then, in 1958, in New Jersey (which was where Gans went to live, to study the phenomenon). Public swimming pools, schools and shops were part of Levitt's instant community package. So were the rules: ready-laid lawns, but no garden fences, to keep the illusion of space. If the lawns weren't mowed, the firm sent a man in, followed by a bill. These new suburbs – which were imitated by many, many others – threw both socialists and elitists into a panic. The folk singer Pete Seeger wrote 'Little Boxes' (recorded on the *Broadside Ballads* album, 1963): 'All built of ticky-tacky, and they all look just the same.' At the other end of the socio-political spectrum, the ultra-metropolitan novelist Gore Vidal, in a 1966 essay on pornography for the *New York Review of Books*, perceived even darker threats. In contemporary literature, he reckoned, 'The decline of incest as a marketable theme is probably due to today's inadequate middle class housing. In large Victorian houses with many rooms and heavy doors, the occupants could be mysterious and exciting to one another in a way that those who live in rackety developments can never hope to be. Not even the lust of a Lord Byron could survive the fact of Levittown.' Well, maybe so.

Levittown, New Jersey (now renamed Willingboro), a much-maligned prototype of US suburban expansion after the Second World War. But Levittowns worked, and were the focus of H.J. Gans's pioneering sociological study in 1967. Aerial view, early 1960s: a middle school being built in foreground.

Above: The interior of a Levittown New Jersey model home. Left: Opening day, 1958.

Gans decided the time had come to rescue 'a much maligned part of America, suburbia,' he wrote. 'The postwar suburban developments, of which the Levittowns are undoubtedly the prototype, have been blamed for many of the country's alleged and real ills, from destroying its farmland to emasculating its husbands.' Gans lived in the New Jersey Levittown for the first two years of its existence, from 1958–60. He found, as Peter Willmott did in Dagenham, that all the lineaments of a genuine community, with its loves and hates, its hopes and its despondencies, duly emerged. The precise design of a house matters much less than professional architects think. Years later, writing in 1991 about Edge City, and the houses, offices and other structures which grew up around out-of-town malls, Joel Garreau decided that the only way to find out what was going on was to talk to real estate people, developers and salesmen. Architects knew nothing at all, he felt.

To me, when it was published in 1967, Gans's study was such a revelation that, at the magazine where I then worked, I cleared the centre pages in order to print extracts. How people actually lived was much more important than the way other people thought they lived, or should live. I had read Michael Young and Peter Willmott's sociological study of Bethnal Green, *Family and Kinship in East London*, when my family and I were living in Stepney (now part of the borough of Tower Hamlets). I had been very taken by the descriptions of East End life in the 1950s, though I was also very conscious of what was left out. For example, there was hardly any mention of crime at a time when the Kray brothers were alive and well and racketeering. Nor did Jewishness feature much, even though the East End was still a focus for British Judaism. The younger generation had mostly left, but other Jews, older or poorer or both, were living where they had grown up. Many local firms and shops were Jewish-run. Orthodox Jews would sometimes ask my wife or me, being *goyim*, to put on their house lights on a Friday evening as the Sabbath began. The Orthodox prohibition against lighting fires on the Sabbath included electric switches.

But what dismayed me most in Young and Willmott's study were their chapters on the new council-house suburb of 'Greenleigh' (in fact, Debden, in Essex), to which some Bethnal Greeners had moved. Here, the old sad song about the suburbs was sung. Young and Willmott regretted that the shopping centre at the parade had displaced the old street-barrows. The chimes of the ice cream van had ousted the one-time barrel organ. When a family sat around their television, the authors mused, 'The scene had the air of a strange ritual.'

Contrariwise, as David Edgerton could have pointed out, Greenleigh/ Debden was a form of organic growth. It was an example of what the urban historian Mark Clapson has called 'the invincible green suburbs'. It was also an example of the shock of the old: carrying on, and mildly changing, something that had been demonstrated to work. It was a 1950s continuation of the interwar passion for suburban living. The Young and Wilmott criticisms (amended later by Willmott in his Dagenham study) echoed the interwar diagnoses of something called 'suburban neurosis'. The term was invented by a London hospital doctor, Stephen Taylor, in a paper in *The Lancet* in 1938. Looked back at today, the paper is amazingly short of analysis, but long on social prejudice. Like many other male critics of suburbia, Dr Taylor seemed to be especially worried by the effect on women – in particular, on 'young hussies who work in biscuit factories'. His big problem seems to have been the new freedoms of suburbia. These young women should have stuck with Victorian or Edwardian tradition, and helped to swell the shrinking interwar pool of domestic servants, working for (let's say) deserving GPs. Later, Taylor became a Labour MP and, eventually, a life peer. His 'diagnosis' was often repeated. As a phrase it was a clever invention. It was soon to be followed by the discovery of 'New Town blues'. Neither illness now crops up much in the records of doctors' twenty-first-century group practices.

Meanwhile, the architectural profession galloped off in pursuit of the shock of the new. For landmark buildings, this was, in its own way, traditional. It followed in the footsteps of the classic engineers: the men who built the great train sheds and the great bridges. In London, Reyner Banham remarked that the Post Office Tower (now the BT Tower), which was pure engineering, was the only new tall structure which deserved to share the skyline with Wren's St Paul's. The record with civic and educational structures was less good. The materials favoured by the Modern movement – glass and bare concrete – seldom performed well, in the long term, in Britain's damp and cold. Curtain walling was better in theory than in practice. And Modernists proved to be very unskilled at producing an alternative set of symbols to those that an older tradition of architecture had evolved. Compare any town hall built before 1939 with any built since.

Even universities, which gave employment to many architectural firms from the 1960s onwards, found it hard to come up with designs that embodied what the campus thought it was there for. Paradoxically, one of the most enduringly attractive designs in Britain was that for the University of York, which put its money into fine landscaping. For everything else, it used the cheap CLASP system, originally exploited in Hertfordshire for quick-build primary schools. This story has much in common with the postwar prefabricated bungalows, erected during a mysterious brick shortage in the late 1940s. The prefabs, which were much liked by their tenants, and the University of York buildings, proved again the old French rule that *il n'y a que le provisoire qui dure*: the only things that last are those which were meant to be temporary.

In housing, the pursuit of the new was a disaster. It was mainly a disaster for the occupants of public housing. A tiny number of private clients ordered new homes, in the new style, for themselves. A high proportion of these clients were the architects' parents, in-laws or friends. Sometimes, the architects commissioned themselves – acting as do-it-yourself clients. On the whole, however, architects continued with their long-established Modernist habit of seldom living in the kinds of house they built for others. They usually preferred something Georgian or Victorian, in a fashionable – or, at least, up-and-coming – part of town.

In the case of spec-built suburbia, the question 'Who is the client?' was simple enough. It was the kind of person who wanted to take out a mortgage on what the developer was offering. In the case of public housing – which, in theory, Modernist architects regarded as one of the main criteria of their success – the question 'Who is the client?' dissolved in a fog of bureaucracy and muddle. Much of the funding came from the state, most of the management came from the local authority, most of the money was made by big building firms who had honed their expertise on huge wartime projects, and hadn't drawn from them the same humane lesson as Levitt. But the architects, who have since tried to pass on the blame to other pieces in the jigsaw, created the designs. It is true, for example, that in 1950s Britain the Housing Ministry decided to skew state subsidies in favour of tall blocks. They were supposed to be cheaper to build, and to save on land. These sums left out of account the cost of maintenance and the huge amount of blank, empty land required around each tall block.

These failings eventually became all too clear. But at the time few architects complained. There was nothing inevitable about the outcomes. Most local authorities followed the instructions of the state planners, but not all of them. The taller the block the greater the advertisement for the architects, many of whom at that time worked in local authority offices themselves. When the fashion shifted towards slightly lower blocks, linked by concrete decking, the results were just as tough on the tenants. Many tenants thought they had been blessed when their run-down Victorian terraces were demolished – even though subsequent evidence showed that almost all these could have been rehabilitated at little cost – and they moved into brand-new flats with bathrooms that worked and nice, modern heating systems. They were rapidly disillusioned.

Le Corbusier is often blamed for what went wrong. It is true that he was the most forceful advocate of a single programme of architectural ideals since Pugin and Ruskin. All three men believed that a specific form of architecture – French gothic for Pugin, Venetian gothic for Ruskin, Modernism for Le Corbusier – could, in itself, bring about a new, improved society. But Le Corbusier's designs for houses were mostly for single dwellings. The big exception was his Unité d'Habitation block at Marseilles. When he sketched his dictatorial Voisin Plan for Paris, which implied the demolition of much of the central city, and scattering it with tall blocks, these were intended as offices, not houses. But that was not how Le Corbusier was read, especially in Britain.

The great propagandists, in Britain, of a new architecture of housing were Peter and Alison Smithson. Peter Smithson was an authoritative and, by all accounts, authoritarian teacher at the Architectural Association in London from the 1950s onwards. 'To those who did not know them well,' one obituarist wrote, 'they could appear a somewhat forbidding couple – an impression fostered in part by the fact that they seldom smiled in photographs.' They influenced an entire generation of architects. Peter Smithson, because of his sternness and rigour, was nicknamed 'Brutus'. The *Oxford Dictionary of Architecture* suggested, slyly, that the name 'brutalism' for the kind of architecture they advocated derived partly from this in-joke, and not only from the Smithsons' advocacy of *beton brut* (raw, exposed concrete), as favoured by Le Corbusier in many of his later buildings.

Top: A 'street in the sky', at Park Hill, Sheffield. Above: The would-be model, Bethnal Green c.1950, photographed by Nigel Henderson.

Raw concrete looks better in strong sunlight than in countries like Britain or Sweden with cloudier skies and plenty of rain. Once, interviewing Denys Lasdun, architect of the National Theatre, I hinted that the theatre, and the adjacent Hayward Gallery, would look much better, in a London context, if the water-stained raw concrete exteriors were covered with stucco and painted cream or white. Lasdun was very offended. All would be well, he responded, if only the theatre exterior was properly maintained and regularly cleaned. The last thing any public body has the money for is extensive cleaning. The historical way round this was to design a surface which was self-cleaning or very easily re-painted.

Intriguingly, it is usually acknowledged that the Smithsons' own best building – many would say their only good building – was that which they built for the *Economist* magazine in St James's in 1962–4. The Pevsner entry makes it clear how much of the inspiration came from the *Economist*

management and even from the contractors. The Smithsons found they had a client just as rigorous as themselves. Geoffrey Crowther, chairman of the *Economist*, wanted a Modernist building. But he also wanted one which fitted into its St James's surroundings, and would look good year in and year out. The Smithsons yielded, and the building is finished with a fossil-rich variety of Portland stone, known as roach. This was true luxury. The upshot was, as the Pevsner guide remarks, 'one of the few 1960s precincts to have stood the test of time'. It was also the first 1960s work to be conservation-listed, in 1988.

That was one kind of architecture, with a clear-minded, determined client, who had money. It was not the architecture the Smithsons spent their professional life advocating. (They played down the *Economist* building in their publications, as if somehow ashamed of its non-puritanism. I could find no mention of it in their 1970 book *Ordinariness and Light*.) Sometimes teachers wonder what influence they actually have on their students. For better or worse, the case of the Smithsons should reassure them.

The phrase the Smithsons came up with, as their big idea for new public housing, was 'the building as street', otherwise known as 'streets in the sky'. To their credit, they saw the shortcomings of the free-standing tower block.

Park Hill was the first built example of Peter and Alison Smithsons' big idea for new public housing. They despised suburbia. The estate was erected in 1957–61 and the dilemma of how to humanise it remains. Compare and contrast the Levittowns (pages 112–13).

But their alternative was no better. For the unfortunate inhabitants, it was in some ways worse.

Inevitably, the Smithsons despised suburbia. *Ordinariness and Light* has what I take to be the characteristic Smithson tone: a mixture of assertion and rhetoric, but little empathy or imagination. 'The argument that suburbs are what people want is invalid,' they pronounced. They sneer at the love of gardens, and at 'the simple well-wishers, of the back-to-gentle-nature era'. They praise Le Corbusier's 1930 plans for the city of Algiers, with its long lines of high-rise terraces – the clear origin of their own 'streets in the sky': 'Why are we forever going up and down, and along and up again, when we could all live on a quiet street-deck for pedestrians, young children, milkmen's trolleys, prams?' A photograph of rows of Lancashire by-law housing in Burnley – solid and durable, even if not especially beautiful – was included in order to show the evil and naivety of the old ways. 'It is the idea of a street, not the reality of a street, that is important.' A high-rise design, preferably in raw concrete, could be linked by long wide terraces, and all would be well. With such a design, 'vertical living becomes a reality. The refuse chute takes the place of the village pump.' A photograph of the long houses of the Sea Dyaks in New Guinea showed the way forward: 'Some houses are a quarter of a mile long and hold 90 families.'

The aggressiveness towards other people's wishes is extraordinary. 'Spiritually dead houses [presumably like those Burnley nineteenth-century terraces] can be bulldozed into contour relief, ready for our new homes to look at.' A photograph of a Levittown is presented as yet another version of architectural evil. Photography seems often to have been their inspiration. The photographer Nigel Henderson portrayed street life in Bethnal Green at about the same time as Young and Willmott were carrying out their sociological work. His photographs now look like something from another world. But they were a big influence on the Smithsons. This sense of urban togetherness, they judged, would be recreated by their planned elevated walkways, with access to the flats on one side.

Their own best shot at achieving this was Robin Hood Gardens, in Poplar, east London. Crammed into an unwelcoming location, overlooking the Blackwall tunnel entry road, it made the site worse, not better. This was the unfortunate East End performing again its long-time role as guinea pig.

I walked down Poplar High Street, in the shadow of Canary Wharf, to reach the Smithsons' nightmare creation. Along the street, a few simple but elegant nineteenth-century houses had survived the bombers and the planners. There were some modest two- and three-storey council flats. Then: Robin Hood Gardens. It was like two long seven-storey workhouses, facing each other. The balconies were narrow and shrouded with netting to stop children falling off or objects being thrown down. The flats themselves were crammed to the edges of the site with a huge waste space in the middle. Bits of landscaping – for example, a 'comic' serpent, a playground and a soccer pitch – didn't counter the bleakness. All the concrete was rain-stained. The tenants seemed mostly

The child in the city: two ways to play. Below left: Heygate estate, Southwark, south London, built in 1970–4, with 1,194 'dwellings'. Below right : Milton Keynes, 1980s.

to be Asian, to judge by the curtain material. All the doors were electronically controlled, in a poor man's version of a gated community. There was no shop or pub, though a notice announced that there was, somewhere, an over-60s club.

The London County Council is often praised (by architects) for its architectural achievements. Over-praised, rather. Robin Hood Gardens, on which building work began in 1966, was one of the LCC's final commissions. The tenants soon started to complain about water leaking into the flats, and moved out if they possibly could. The burglary rate was twenty times the London council-house norm. The 'streets in the sky' were wonderful rat-runs for thieves, drug dealers and vandals. In his last book, *The Charged Void* (2001), Peter Smithson included a picture of Robin Hood Gardens the day they were completed – not what became of them in use. To go there was to see a tombstone to progressive public housing. The Smithsons themselves lived in a Victorian house in Chelsea. All too characteristically, the Commission for Architecture and the Built Environment resisted the sensible proposal in 2008 that Robin Hood Gardens should be demolished, in favour of homes people might actually enjoy living in.

The Smithsons' only other building of note was a school at Hunstanton in Norfolk, built in 1950–4 with no thought either for the use children might make of it, or for the local climate. There was so much glass it was freezing cold in winter and uncomfortably hot in summer. All the spaces opened on to one another. Curtains had to be put up in the hall, to give some privacy. Dining room smells permeated everywhere. The steel framing warped because no expansion joints had been designed in. Glass popped out of its frames. The Pevsner guide to Norfolk describes the school as 'a maintenance headache in a class of its own'. Most teachers hated it. It was an experiment never repeated.

Unfortunately, the streets-in-the-sky dogma was repeated over and over again, throughout British cities. In south London, for example, attractive 'gingerbread' Victorian terraces were demolished in favour of such grim concrete monstrosities as the deck-access Aylesbury estate. This policy was boldly attacked by the maverick architecture writer Nicholas Taylor. His long-standing criticisms were encapsulated in his polemical book *The Village in the City* (1973). When Tony Blair became Prime Minister, he chose the Aylesbury estate, built in 1967–77, as the backdrop for his 1997 photo-opportunity announcement of his new government's social policies. When he left office in 2007, the estate was still standing. And away from the eyes of the national press, in Liverpool and other northern towns and cities, the Blair and Brown governments had reverted to the idea that the only thing to do with shabby, but solid nineteenth-century terraces was to pull them down.

The idea that a community can be instantly created, or recreated, was one of the many flaws behind 'streets in the sky'. Two of the Smithsons' most ardent followers were the architects Hugh Wilson and Lewis Womersley. Wilson created the disastrous town centre block at Cumbernauld New Town, in central Scotland. In Sheffield, Womersley, as city architect, designed the notorious Park Hill estate. This was erected in 1957–61 as the first built expression of the Smithson credo. It was later joined by a similarly inspired but even more titanic neighbour, the Hyde Park estate. In spite of the usual semi-sociological justifications, Park Hill did not reflect the actual street life of Sheffield, which was based on the court, rather than the street. In any event, the existing houses had mostly been cleared, so there was no existing community left to move into the new flats. The core of the Hyde Park estate was demolished in 1992. The dilemma of how to humanise Park Hill remained.

In Manchester, Wilson and Womersley joined forces to do everything they could to destroy an entire district. They were the city's evil genies. Their firm created streets in the sky for the inner-city district of Hulme. This had been cleared by Manchester city council in the 1950s and 1960s. It was claimed, at the time, to be the largest redevelopment area in Europe. Manchester city council commissioned Wilson and Womersley to fill the gap. The centrepiece was four six-storey deck-access 'crescents', each a quarter of a mile long. Hubristically, the crescents were named after historic stars in the architectural firmament, Robert Adam, John Nash, William Kent and Charles Barry. Completed in 1971, this became rapidly one of the worst estates in Europe: a spectacular failure. A new round of demolition began in 1991. This meant that the local community had also been also demolished twice in forty years. A new Hulme was begun, with an attempt to restore old street lines and build more humanely. The jury is still out. When I walked round, it was clear that many of the houses were being lived in by the poor. Could a new ghetto be avoided? Would it have been any worse to cover the site with spec-built pebbledash semis and bungalows? Or would that have taken the shock of the old too far?

7. SHOPPING AROUND

When I first went to the MetroCentre mall, at Gateshead, I was enchanted by its ordinariness. This was the first ever shopping mall of the full-blown American kind to be opened in Britain. Naturally, it had precursors. Nothing comes from nowhere. At Milton Keynes – a town, as always, ahead of its time – a long central mall was planned in from the start. It was intended to be a new version of a city centre. Built on MK's Midsummer Boulevard in 1973–7, the 'Shopping Centre' wasn't air-conditioned and you could walk through it, unsupervised, at any time of day or night, as if it were a street. The avowed model, at the time, wasn't the United States – in spite of the acknowledged American influence on the New Town's layout – but Europe's nineteenth-century glass-covered arcades, most notably Milan's Galleria. British architects have a recurrent yearning to make Britain more Mediterranean. This has seldom worked out well. If you now go to the Shopping Building – renamed The Centre, MK – you'll see it has been fitted with air conditioning, the usual doors and guards, and it shuts at night.

In north London, the shopping centre at Brent Cross, on the North Circular Road, was always nearer to the American model. Built in 1970–6, it was Britain's first air-conditioned mall. (The first in the world had opened in Milwaukee in 1956, one year after the first McDonalds.) Brent Cross began with 3,600 parking places, and soon acquired many more. But, as first built, it was still small compared to the American malls. More comparable, in fact, to superstores like Carrefour and Leclerc, which were already adorning the edge of French towns and cities. The French are always keen verbally to distance themselves from the United States, but they were the European pioneers of placing malls and retail strips on all the urban outskirts. The numerous Britons who have bought second homes in France admire the specialist shops in French town centres, but they always do their weekly shopping at the superstore.

MetroCentre opened in 1986. A power station ash dump was wasteland until a local developer, John Hall, spotted the benefits of the tax and planning breaks that the Thatcher government offered to the various Enterprise Zones, and built his mall. (In London, another Enterprise Zone, in Docklands, gave

Opposite: Kurt Geiger luxury shoe shop in The Glades mall, Bromley.

birth to Canary Wharf.) The next mall off the production line was Sheffield's Meadowhall. From the M1 you look down on Meadowhall's green dome, enveloped in parked cars, in the old wasteland of the lower Don valley. On the other side of the M1, heritage campaigners battled to keep, as landmarks, two huge electricity cooling stations that dominated that stretch of motorway. They got nowhere. Off with the old, on with the new. Sheffielders were more interested in the Meadowhall landmark. The mall's brochures told you that this bit of south Yorkshire was written up by Sir Walter Scott in the first paragraph of *Ivanhoe*. More to the point, the lower Don valley was the home of the gigantic Hadfield steel firm. That era of industrial history ended in blood and tears in the first great union battle of the Thatcher years. In 1980, during a British Steel Corporation strike, mass picketing outside Hadfield's East Hecla works led to scores of arrests. Three years later, the last Hadfield's works closed, and the land became derelict. A parable of our time. At the new mall, Warner built an eleven-screen multiplex. And where did Sheffield decide to put its first super-tram line? From the old city centre to Meadowhall.

In her comprehensive history, *English Shops and Shopping*, Kathryn Morrison, of English Heritage, argued in 2003 that 'In the short space of forty years, the fickle world of shopping had been transformed with greater rapidity than at any other time in history.' Ten years earlier, in 1993, when John Gummer, as Environment Secretary, was battling to prevent the construction of any more out-of-town malls, his planning decree nonetheless stated: 'It is not the role of the planning system to restrict competition, preserve existing commercial interests or to prevent innovation.' As always, social trends have a tendency to eddy around whatever restrictions are laid on them. Kathryn Morrison correctly foresaw that the immediate result would be to cause developers to switch to hefty *in-town* malls, like The Oracle in the middle of Reading, or Westfield at Shepherds Bush in west London. (Was this what the malls' opponents really had in mind?) And the big superstore owners, like Sainsbury or Tesco, decided to invade the high streets with smaller, late-opening convenience stores. They were going back to the stores' origins, when Jack Cohen, founder of Tesco, said his magic motto was 'Pile 'em high, sell 'em cheap'. This gave rise to yet another outcry from preservationists. When Tesco, Sainsbury and Marks & Spencer opened such shops near where I live, I noticed that the outcry quickly faded. Ex-preservationists queued up at the check-out like everyone else. I asked a long-established florist, near the Tesco, whether the new shop had hit his business. He carried on wrapping tulips and said: 'Yes, to begin with. But now we sell more than we ever did. We put out more varied bunches on the pavement, ready to just pick up, and we offer more options all round. Probably it was all a good thing, a bit of competition. It gave us a kick up the pants.' I don't think he was simply putting on a brave face. His wife, busy making up a special order, nodded agreement. 'Tesco seem to be winding down their flower section,' she said.

Elsewhere, in the case of the malls, you have to remember the crumminess of much of what they supposedly destroyed. If your alternative were to shop in Sunderland's depressing high street or in the squalid shopping precinct at Peterlee New Town, you too would go to MetroCentre, Gateshead. If a town centre is good enough, it does not succumb. The shopping heart of Newcastle-upon-Tyne beat vigorously, in spite of MetroCentre across the Tyne.

Asda supermarket checkout, Stevenage New Town, Hertfordshire.

All the same, cities are being turned inside out. Edge City has arrived. The retail parks continue to spring up about the periphery, even if the biggest out-of-town shopping malls have been put on hold since the baroque splendours of the Trafford Centre, outside Manchester (1998) and Bluewater, in a north Kent quarry (1999). Before we rush to praise or blame, we must try to grasp exactly what is happening. In the early twenty-first century, it is as important to understand Edge City as it was for Friedrich Engels, in the early nineteenh century, to try to understand the cotton capital, Manchester. Greater understanding will perhaps lead to less bossiness. Many planners, both professional and amateur, very quickly fall into a we-know-best way of talking, and acting. It is always wiser to remember that other people have preferences of their own, and usually for good reason. Tolerance is the best policy. Happiness is best served by allowing people to pursue their own interests their own way. And their personal choices may even turn out to be the right ones.

If the malls and the superstores were a superfluous invention, they would have gone the way of the pogo stick and the hula hoop. Instead, they are with us, not forever, but for many decades to come.

It is extraordinary how the social geography of cities, across the industrialised world, falls into similar patterns – at greater or less speed – in spite of widely divergent histories, politics and planning systems. The malls are emblems of a deep shift in economics and behaviour. The car and the motorway are the generating forces. Often the out-of-town stores pretend to be brick-built barns. But why not pretend? The first cars looked like a pony-and-trap, minus the pony. The first television sets had little doors to make them look like veneered china cabinets. The first railway stations and their hotels pretended to be mansions, town halls or, as at St Pancras, amazing Mervyn Peake castles.

Many observers of what is happening in and around British cities, and especially in and around London, panic as they look at these dark satanic malls. (The cotton mills of Lancashire are probably not what Blake originally had in mind. But they are certainly how generations of singers of 'Jerusalem' saw, and felt, the poem's imagery. They are now the subject of preservation orders.) Cities are, of their nature, ever-changing. Or, if they are not, they are dead. This museumised fate appears to be overtaking Paris, as traditionally defined (that is, inside the *périphérique* road). If you see a French film of the 1950s, such as Jules Dassin's heist movie *Rififi* (1955), it is a revelation to see how little the background of inner Paris has changed in more than fifty years. Compare this static townscape with a British film such as *The Long Good Friday* (1979), where Bob Hoskins and Helen Mirren play an east London gangster and his moll. The dockland London, which is the setting for much of the film, is all but unrecognisable thirty years later.

Cities are anarchic. The living city is forever 'in crisis'. That is one way you can tell that it is alive. Those who find this appalling (and attractive) vigour unacceptable would like to stop change in its tracks. Human nature being what it is, they would often like to stop it at the point where they themselves benefit most. When they look at the retail-driven growth of Edge City – all those car parks, those glittering domes, those gushing fountains – they thrown up their hands, yet again, at the horrors that suburbanites commit. And, inevitably, these horrid things are all 'American'. So are innumerable novelties. For the time being, the United States still operates as the global innovation centre. In tribute to Britain's nineteenth-century predominance, the country's postage stamps are the only ones that carry no explicit national identification. The only nation whose email addresses carry no comparable identification is the United States.

In his original plans for a garden city, published in 1898, Ebenezer Howard surrounded the town centre with an enormous ring-like glazed arcade. He called it the 'Crystal Palace,' in homage to Joseph Paxton's Hyde Park design for the 1851 Great Exhibition, by then re-located in south London. More importantly, like much of his thinking (including the name 'garden city'), it sprang from his experience of working in Nebraska and Chicago in the 1870s. Chicago was an enormously energetic place. The energy, at that time, was expressed architecturally in Beaux Arts magnificence, and socially in a hucksterish bumptiousness. Howard's explanatory diagram for his garden city resembled a Beaux Arts plan, comparable to that for the exuberant Chicago World's Fair of 1893. Howard's description of his proposed (but unbuilt) arcade is worth reproducing. No mall promoter could have put it better:

> This building is in wet weather one of the favourite resorts of the people. . . . Here manufactured goods are exposed for sale, and here most of that class of shopping which requires the joy of deliberation and selection is done.

Chicago was to be the birthplace of the skyscraper, and of great stores like Marshall Field, whose vast warehouse of 1885–7 made Henry Richardson's name as an architect. The department store, open to all, was an American invention. (Earlier stores always had a man at the door to keep out the great unwashed, and a male floorwalker to guide the respectable female customers from display to display.) Gordon Selfridge transferred the American idea to England. He saw a big store as a 'retail theatre'. Mohammed Fayed, the eccentric owner of Harrods, was just such a showman.

Confronted with these innovations, the architecture critics of the day disliked what they saw, just as their successors disliked the malls. The Dickens & Jones department store on Regent Street, now rejigged to hold the British flagship store of the US Banana Republic chain, opened for business in 1922. *Country Life* commented sniffily that the violently eclectic façade was 'like the finale of some old-fashioned musical comedy when all the company collected on the stage and waved flags and kicked legs and climbed rostrums while the orchestra rose from din to din'. (This must mean the sort of candy-floss show you could see all over the West End before the all-conquering arrival of Jerome Kern's *Showboat*, starring Paul Robeson, in 1928.)

The malls unashamedly follow an American line of descent. As Kathryn Morrison points out: 'All fashionable retail formats eventually lose their sparkle.' The novelties can take surprising forms. Which is the point of them. Newness sells. The Woolworth nickel and dime store became the threepenny and sixpenny store in Britain, starting in 1909 at the then-prosperous port of Liverpool, where the transatlantic liners docked. The reshaping of old fruit and vegetable wholesale markets, like Covent Garden, as 'festival malls' had its origin in America in the 1970s, especially at Boston's Quincy Market. In the 1990s, farmers' markets were another idea imported from America. At the one end of the contemporary Anglo-American spectrum is Wal-Mart ('Always low prices'), with its British subsidiary Asda. At the other end, organic duck eggs. 'After 1945,' Morrison notes, 'American influence governed all.' Thus was created a new landscape of desire.

In the attacks on this, the great English vice of snobbery plays a big part. Derision of the brazenly populist designs of the shopping malls follows in the footsteps of the earlier onslaughts on 1920s suburban semis or 1930s supercinemas, on 1950s TV aerials or on 1980s satellite dishes. The motto often

seems to be: Find out what those people are doing, and tell them to stop it. Especially if they are enjoying it. Yet, a generation later, nostalgia always sets in. What was despised becomes 'heritage'. (Except among those who also despise 'heritage' as having, itself, become too populist.) There was so much public nostalgia when the last Woolworth stores closed in 2008–9 that you thought the National Trust might move in. You dare not today pull down an Art Deco cinema, but you may well decide to convert it from its grey half-life as a bingo hall into a fancy gastro-pub. Or, to put it another way, from working class to middle class.

Why do the new malls arouse such anger? Why do they produce, among some, a desire to force people back, somehow into the kind of shopping they have abandoned? I found myself in an environmentalist discussion group after I had visited Poundbury, Prince Charles's pleasant garden suburb on the edge of Dorchester (built on 'greenfield' land, as it happens). All the inhabitants I spoke

Town-edge Tesco, Dorchester, Dorset: a pastiche of a late-Victorian town hall or chapel. On the town by-pass, this is where people in Prince of Wales's neo-classical Poundbury village – master-planner Leon Krier – drive to shop.

even thought of. Once upon a time, to own a small shop was a classic way out of the working class. But it was gruelling work. After shopfloor wages rose and hours were cut, why should anyone risk that way of life? Where I grew up in the Yorkshire Pennines, there were a dozen small shops, including a Co-op and two fish and chip shops within a five-minute walk of where I lived – and this was not even the town centre. These shops began to close down in the 1950s. All have gone.

It is wrong to see malls as mere parodies of traditional cities. I have already quoted Jane Jacobs on personal safety as the 'bedrock attribute of a successful city'. Enclosed and video-scrutinised, the malls make people, especially women, feel safer. The malls' success, first in the United States, then in Britain and elsewhere, is inseparable from the upsurge in women going out to work and the all but inevitable arrival of the family's second car. In 2008, the Joseph Rowntree Trust carried out a survey of living costs. One of its less impressive findings was that a car was a 'luxury', as opposed to such 'necessities' as a DVD player, a mobile phone and an annual holiday away from home. What world do such researchers live in?

Campaigners weep for high street shops. But there are simply too many of them for the present-day demand. They should be allowed to revert to other uses, including housing. Look at old photographs, and you will see that many were built into or on to street-side houses. Today nothing is more depressing than a row of charity shops interspersed with estate agents' 'To Let' signs.

Streets lined with shops selling everyday necessities were a nineteenth-century invention. New national retail chains soon emerged, like the Home & Colonial Stores (the profits from whose groceries went into building Lutyens's Castle Drogo in Devon) or Dewhurst the Butchers (the profits from whose frozen New Zealand lamb and Argentine beef went into building the central tower of Liverpool's Anglican cathedral). These chain stores, in their day, were also derided by the intelligentsia, as destroying the 'traditional' high street. One of these chains was J. Sainsbury, originally of Drury Lane, but soon of almost every high street in the south-east of England. Unlike many others, Sainsbury's is still with us. The firm adapted.

Before the nineteenth century, shops were only there for specialist services for the well-to-do: hatters, milliners, tailors, wine merchants, booksellers. The world of Mrs Gaskell's Cranford. Everyday goods were bought at markets. Against all predictions, the love of markets has outlived the love of high street shops. The car boot sale is at one end of this passion, the mall is at the other. In essence, a mall is an indoor market, in direct line of descent from Victorian arcades.

The mall's other parent is the funfair. When I came in from the bus station at MetroCentre, on my first visit, I reached 'Metroland'. You could buy a day ticket for your children. A friendly dragon floated over the entrance. A rollercoaster whooshed overhead. A ferris wheel turned. A toy train clanged its bell without ceasing. The din was all very satisfactory.

The English landscape is an artificial construction, strewn with the dry-stone walling of parliamentary enclosure, the architectural follies of the aristocracy, the pylons of the electricity grid and the reservoirs of the city water boards. And now the malls, calmly awaiting their first conservation listing.

Bluewater mall (page 135) targets prosperous shoppers, and seeks to outbid Bromley and even Bond Street. But Lakeside (opposite), a few miles away across the Queen Elizabeth II Thames bridge, clings to its east London roots. This market stall is inside the mall itself, not tucked away.

8. A SPACE OF ONE'S OWN

'That is well said,' Candide remarked, 'but we must cultivate our garden.' On the road up to Epping Forest, I drove through the north-east London suburb of Walthamstow. After the railway reached here in 1870, aspirant East End families moved in, in droves, tempted by cheap land and cheap rail tickets to and from Liverpool Street station. All around me were the little Victorian gingerbread houses, sometimes in semis, sometimes in terraces (if so, the doors were paired). I saw ahead, and to the right, the bright white Portland stone town hall. It always stuns unwary passers-by as they drive along Forest Road (otherwise known as the A503), through the surrounding shabbiness, on their way out to the M11 or M25.

Albert Speer built like this. So did many of Stalin's architects. The town hall reminded me of Osbert Lancaster's clever cartoon image of Soviet and Nazi monumental architecture, indistinguishable but for the rival over-blown emblems above the facades. This grandiose structure was erected just before the Second World War, to trumpet the progressive-mindedness of Walthamstow's Labour council. Attlee, later the party's most admired Prime Minister, is said to have come to the opening. The matching assembly hall, alongside the town hall, has enormous carved lettering across its cornice. This says, not *Arbeit Macht Frei* or Workers of the World Unite, but 'Fellowship is Life and the Lack of Fellowship is Death.'

'It only needs a red banner and a swastika, doesn't it?' said the man bending over his peas in the allotments behind the town hall. 'You go about, hoeing and weeding, and you're always conscious of Big Brother watching you.'

The carved quotation comes from William Morris's novel *A Dream of John Ball*. Morris was a Walthamstow lad. His father worked in the City of London, and suddenly died when his business failed. Morris described the Walthamstow he knew as 'a suburban village on the edge of Epping Forest'. You still see the forest on the skyline, beyond the roadside shops which offer 'English and Polish food', cheap drum kits, 'Con Amore sandwiches', ceramic tiling and council-licensed sex items. (For a cup of tea there is Tommy's Tuc Inn Café.) In adulthood Morris

Opposite: Garden lovers. Statuary in a garden centre in D.H. Lawrence's home town, Eastwood, Nottinghamshire.

helped to preserve the forest, which he saw as 'a very curious and characteristic wood, such as can be seen nowhere else'. He had loved gardens from his earliest childhood. He recreated them in his ravishing fabrics and wallpapers. He preferred gardens that mixed the formal with the informal. You could call it the English style. Around the town hall, I saw a social and horticultural schizophrenia. In the front, on the shaven municipal lawns, roses, tulips and wallflowers marched along in regimented lines: as lifeless as plastic soldiers. A huge blue-tiled fountain, its spray sparkling in the sun, reminded me of a mall. But behind the town hall, in the allotments, you had all the charms of anarchy.

The allotment sheds were made from offcuts of wood, old doors, leftover corrugated iron. I walked among the carefully tilled plots. At first glance, everyone seemed to be growing potatoes, beans, turnips and the traditional row of chrysanths. On a closer look, it wasn't quite so. Everyone could deploy their own taste. One man broke off from tying bean strings to show me his garlic, gladioli and geraniums. Another, busy trying to clip his raspberries into quiescence, had various West Indian specialisms coming along: bush marrow, chilli peppers and callaloo.

Afterwards I spent hours trying to find out what callaloo was. I bought a couple of tins of it from a West Indian shop off the Holloway Road, on my way back from Walthamstow. We tried some at home. This only proved that it was rather like spinach, green and a bit sludgy. Callaloo wasn't in my edition of *The Oxford Book of Food Plants* by name. Nor did a couple of friendly botanists come up with an answer, until I posted on to them the picture on the label of one of the tins. This gave a clue. It turned out that callaloo is the name for the leaves of the taro plant, which grows in 'many parts of the wet tropics' (according to its Oxford entry). 'Taro' is the name given to the plant on the Pacific islands where it came from. In the West Indies it is 'dasheen'; in West Africa, 'old cocoyam'. It is mostly eaten for its starch-rich stem-base and tubers, which the Oxford guide's writers compare to arrowroot. And now here it was, in north-east London, grown for its leaves. Thus the web of empire spread.

Musing over a cigarette in his allotment, an ex-postman, retired through illness, poured out another cup of tea from his kettle. He had an old enamelled bath filled with manure. He had cut out a big black cat from hardboard as a bird-scarer, with staring mirror-glass eyes. A large box was labelled 'Wormery'. 'Without worms you get a desert,' he told me. He gathered the worms here,

Mutual aid in practice. Allotments like these survive despite numerous pressures.

then put them back into the ground at the right moment. 'Not many people still do this,' he said. I was sure he was right.

Almost all allotment holders are men, but here six women had plots. One of them was struggling, in the chilly wind, to tame her weed-filled garden. Weeds are the biggest impetus for mutual aid among plot holders. No one wants next door's thistle seeds.

The suburban shed culture of allotments has been a gentle part of the British landscape for a couple of hundred years. The plot holders told me they came to these allotments for a mixture of motives: 'to get away from the wife' (crash repair man), 'to take the stress out, especially when I was the shop steward' (typesetter), 'because you can hear a pin drop' (dustman): the town hall was hefty enough to be a noise barrier against the busy road. But the gardeners often sounded rather embattled. A high metal fence, with anti-climb paint, had had to be put up around the site. A notice warned intruders of a possible £25 fine under the 1922 Allotments Act. 'But the kids even steal the notices.'

The trouble wasn't scrumping. Everyone half-accepted that that was how life was. 'I did it myself,' one man said. (And so did I.) The trouble was the theft of tools and the wrecking of huts. If you put a padlock on, it looked as there was something worth stealing. If you didn't, you had to lug your gardening tools home with you. One elderly gardener showed me his ingenious device for bolting his hut so that it didn't show from the outside. 'I was an engineer in the army, you know.'

Environmentalists applaud the idea of allotments, but the practical consequences of environmentalism are part of the pressure on them. The rival arguments over wind farms, with the Campaign to Protect Rural England lining up against Friends of the Earth – or, less parochially, the battle between preserving rain forests and planting bio-fuel crops – show all too vividly that ecology is not a seamless answer. Ruralist campaigners, who say they wish to preserve the countryside, argue for building even more homes within existing cities. But much of this 'regeneration' hasn't taken place on old factory sites. Such land is often badly poisoned and very expensive to clear. It is much easier for developers, housing associations and councils to target urban green space: playing fields, allotments, small parks, gardens. Being within the city boundaries, all these are mysteriously classified as 'brownfield' sites, and so are okay to tear up. Legal tenure on allotments can be lost in the dust of time. The borough council seized one of this Walthamstow allotment association's other sites, to put houses on it. Developers tried to set gardener against gardener by the lump-sum bribes they offered to individuals to forgo their allotment rights.

I went past the back of the town hall, with its statues of 'Motherhood' and 'Recreation'. Some of the many municipal notices were in six languages now, with the arrival of newer populations. Next to Morris's childhood home, now an Arts & Crafts museum, an old brick shed had been converted into a small Sikh temple, with a bright gilt doorway. The towns the borough is twinned with include St John's, Antigua, and Roseau, Dominica.

I wanted to get to the car boot sale on the other side of the allotments' anti-vandal fence. Among the smell of cheap hamburgers, I dodged between heaps of old LPs (Elvis, Berlioz, Frankie Lane), second-hand shoes and children's games. Next to a hanger of flimsy dresses, I found a table full of old tools: hammers, electric drills – and garden forks. I wondered where the forks came from. To

Car boot sales lay bare what people actually buy for their homes, as opposed to what fashion or design magazines state they ought to buy. William Morris said: 'Have nothing in your house that you do not know to be useful, or believe to be beautiful.' But who is to be the judge?

revive a neglected, but not truly dead, pair of social categories, you could say that the fence marked the dividing line between the respectable and the rough. Would you rather cultivate your garden, or your car boot display? I prefer to see the two sides of the fence as alternative versions of anarchy.

The car boot sale evoked, for me, the historian Deborah Cohen's entertaining and scholarly book, *Household Gods: The British and their Possessions*. Sparked off by her passion for car boot sales and junk shops, she decided to explore what people actually bought for their homes in nineteenth- and twentieth-century Britain, as opposed to what designers and architects thought they ought to buy. She wrote that this meant that she 'delves into the realm of what critics have often disdained as bad taste. Readers will encounter in these pages much more about the ugly and the ephemeral than about the beautiful and the transcendent. . . . A wastepaper basket fashioned from an elephant's foot betrays the aspirations of its Edwardian owners; a decorous Voysey wallpaper pattern that never went into production, by contrast, tells us chiefly about what museums have considered worthy design.' (Voysey, who features in the Walthamstow museum, got his revenge in his omnipresent influence on suburban design.) Flea markets and car boot sales are, Cohen argues, as important as museums in reminding us of the richness of 'material culture', in actual use.

Morris said: 'Have nothing in your house anything that you do not know to be useful, or believe to be beautiful.' But whose idea of beauty? Definitions change. In an anthropological study of rubbish, Michael Thompson traced the route by which the rejected eventually becomes a cult object. He included preferred styles of housing in his scheme of things. He was especially intrigued by the way Islington, built as a solid middle class suburb of Georgian terrace houses, slipped down into slumdom, and then began the slow climb up the social hill into favour and even glamour. In *Taste and Fashion*, James Laver, a curator at the Victoria & Albert Museum, spelled out the fashion process for frocks:

> The same costume will be
> Indecent . . . ten years before its time
> Shameless . . . five years before its time
> Outré (daring) . . . one year before its time
> Smart
> Dowdy . . . one year after its time

Hideous . . . ten years after its time
Ridiculous . . . 20 years after its time
Amusing . . . 30 years after its time
Quaint . . . 50 years after its time
Charming . . . 70 years after its time
Romantic . . . 100 years after its time
Beautiful . . . 150 years after its time

A version of the same list would fit house styles. It is worth remembering that, for decades, the now much-prized Georgian terrace house was regarded as dull and boring. The Victorians merrily demolished such terraces. Morris thought that Georgian Gower Street was so ugly it should be blown up. The writers and painters in the Bloomsbury group settled in these terraces because they were so cheap. It wasn't until 1937, the year after the Adam brothers' Adelphi building on the riverside at Charing Cross was demolished, that a Georgian Group was founded to protect what remained. The Georgian terraces and squares of Islington, unlike most of those in Bloomsbury, had been preserved by poverty and by the dirt from coal-powered trains. This deterred the better-off from living there, and replacing the old designs with something smarter.

In due course, Victorian architecture was also despised. The establishment of the Victorian Society in 1958 marked the start of a new reversal in taste. In 1961, the campaigners didn't manage to prevent the demolition of the Euston Arch, in front of the London rail terminus. But under the chairmanship of Nikolaus Pevsner, backed by Betjeman's advocacy skills, they did narrowly succeed in stopping the Gormenghast frontage of St Pancras station being knocked down. (John Summerson, one of the greatest writers on Georgian architecture, had said he would be happy to see it go.) Be careful, even today, what you despise. The Twentieth Century Society explores even newer avenues of taste. So it goes.

If people have a space of their own, they are very resistant to being told what to do with it. Deborah Cohen's appealing thesis is that life is seldom how designers or architects plan it to be. She shows that this is especially true of British suburbanites. They have an ineradicable tendency to prefer maximalism to minimalism. Aided and abetted by the furnishing trade (Maple's and Waring & Gillow once; IKEA and DFS now), they counter Mies van der Rohe's old Modernist slogan, 'Less is more', with one of their own: 'More is better.' From her devoted trawl through retail and manufacturer records, Cohen reported that one 1930s toy-maker put a stripped-down doll's house on the market: flat roof, plate glass, right angles. It never sold. The firm withdrew it in favour of the usual gabling, pitched roof and pebbledash. This was how things were, and are, in the suburbs – to the despair of smart designers and doctrinaire planners.

Deborah Cohen reproduces two photographs of front rooms in the Cadbury model village of Bournville, which drive home her thesis. Both of the pictures date from the early twentieth century, not long after the earliest model houses went up in this Birmingham suburb near the company's chocolate works. The first photograph shows how the Quaker philanthropists, who ran the Bournville Village Trust, hoped such households would be. Everything emphasises plain living and high thinking: a brick fireplace, with a few carefully chosen ornaments above it; a spindle-backed chair; a rag rug; a single tasteful aspidistra. But the second photograph blows the gaff on how suburban taste really was. In this front room, the brick fireplace has acquired a semi-classical marble front and a huge velvet-draped mirror; the chairs are soft and cosy; the figured carpet is overlaid by rugs; flowers abound, both dried and live. In the inglenook stands a bright white reproduction of the Venus de Milo, about three feet high.

In the mid-1970s, in *Morality and Architecture*, David Watkin attacked those who thought that certain styles of architecture had special ethical, not just aesthetic, merit. But Cohen shows that architecture wasn't the half of it. There was (and is) also a suburban morality of objects. In the eighteenth century, taste was seen as innate, but to the Victorians it became something you could buy at a shop. And as religious evangelism faded, Mammon became a kind of substitute god. Thereafter, 'Things had moral qualities,' Cohen observes; 'possessions made the man.' The Victorians, she argues, 'were the first people to be so closely identified with their belongings'. And, of all countries, this was most true of Britain. From the early nineteenth century, such foreign visitors as Emerson from the United States, Taine from France, and Hermann Muthesius, author of *Das Englische Haus*, from Germany, noted that 'house-pride came to define what it meant to be British'. An American war correspondent wrote that, unlike the French, the Englishman didn't go to a café or restaurant to relax. It was only in his home that he 'liked to take his psychological shoes off'. Today's plethora of glossy magazines and television programmes – on houses, on DIY, and even on the supposed antiques in your attic – prove that the obsession with home remains. Love me, love my kitchen paint.

As the nineteenth century unfurled, house interiors became a kind of domestic funfair or circus. They were also a battleground, between men and women, fought most ferociously in the suburbs. Women won. It helped that the man now took an early train to work, and didn't get back till late, when he couldn't interfere. Some enterprising women invented a new job for themselves: first, as so-called 'lady advisers', writing in the newly founded women's magazines; later, as fully fledged interior decorators. Between the two world wars, Syrie Maugham, the third daughter of the strictly evangelical social reformer Thomas Barnardo, specialised in Hollywood-style white-on-white. Her rival Sibyl Colefax, a friend of Virginia Woolf's, propagandised the country-house idiom. Those interior decorators who weren't female were often gay men. The high-camp Ronald Fleming survived the battle of the Somme, and believed in personalised decor from cradle to grave. Dismayed by the prospect of a varnished oak coffin, he ordered his own to be covered in orange-red velvet with rows of small gilt nails.

Top: Electro-plated nickel silverware from Holborn store, c.1910. Bottom: From the Household Bargains Catalogue, produced by Casement Manufacturing Company, Manchester, c.1925.

But the biggest battlegrounds were the shops and the catalogues, now backed up by websites. Here you could (and still can) buy taste by the yard or the hundredweight. Average incomes in Britain doubled in the last fifty years of Victoria's reign. Shops arose to help people spend. The definition of middle class was widening all the time (as it has continued to). All sections joined the quest for taste. On joining Britain's rather bourgeois royal family, the German-born Princess Mary of Teck was dismayed to find that her husband, the future George V, had bought everything from Maple's department store.

John Maple opened a draper's shop on Tottenham Court Road in 1841. By the 1870s it was a monster emporium, which became one of the sights of London. Homes were

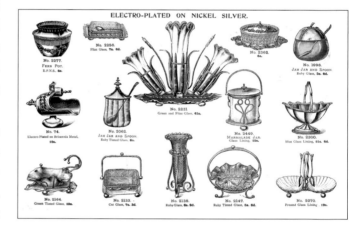

What shall we call it? Top row, left to right: Zadoc, Mayfield Gardens, Staines, Surrey; Water Music, Sandbanks, Poole, Dorset; Valhalla, Staines; Kuala Lumpur, Twickenham, south-west London; Isis, Bromley, south-east London; Thalassa, Peacehaven. Bottom row, left to right: Arden, Swanage, Dorset; Giorgiou's Manor, Jaywick Sands; Dyke Nook, Bingley, west Yorkshire; Lazy Land, Staines; Pixie House, Heronsgate/Charterville.

mocked up in every detail, long before design museums followed suit. There's nothing left of Maple's now, except a street name and the Maple House office block. But on Oxford Street you can still see, slightly to the east of Oxford Circus, the extraordinary Edwardian red-and-white baroque of Waring & Gillow's headquarters store, opened in 1906, and bigger even than Maple's. Now converted to shops and offices, its forty departments covered 40,000 square feet. An average IKEA in Britain runs to 70,000 square feet. But IKEA and the like are assembly lines by comparison. Waring's had a rotunda half the size of St Paul's, adorned with palm trees and Persian rugs.

An evangelical moral passion drove the retailing of taste. 'We are all chameleons; and we take the colour of the objects among which we are placed,' a Scottish parson wrote in 1861. In *Middlemarch*, George Eliot saw Mrs Bulstrode striving to combine 'piety and worldliness, the nothingness of this life with the desirability of cut glass'. Objects were credited with characters, even souls, of their own. In *The Spoils of Poynton* (1897), Henry James chronicles how an antiques collection precipitates a family tragedy. In C.S. Lewis's *The Lion, the Witch and the Wardrobe* (1950), the wardrobe is as important a player as the other two. In 1953, Marghanita Laski published a ghost story, *The Victorian Chaise-longue* (reprinted 1999), in which a woman falling asleep on this item awakens to a phantasmagoria of horror.

Cohen's illustrations reveal how shops and their customers brushed aside the sparseness, and truth to materials that men like William Morris advocated. Gutta-percha, a resin made from latex, was the wonder-material – the polypropylene – of its day. The veneering trade flourished. Paradoxically, the plain Arts & Crafts styles proved the easiest to mass-manufacture. Art Nouveau took its name from a Paris shop. The pioneer of female suffrage Emmeline Pankhurst made various failed attempts to try her hand as a furniture shop owner. At the height of the hunger-strike militancy, in 1911, her journal *Votes for Women* stated that 'No one is more keen about the house than a Suffragette.'

The demise of great department stores like Maple's and Waring & Gillow began just as they seemed most dominant. On high streets, chain stores opened, selling factory-made furniture from shops much nearer to suburban homes. Now there is a mall somewhere within easy driving distance, selling the newest version of the domestic ethic, affordable by more people than ever before. Add to this the influence of the garden centre, selling more and more lifestyle seeds and plants.

The British home and garden is still a display case for moral and aesthetic values, as demonstrated by what you've bought. Suburbia has won the battle of taste.

By some reckonings, Birmingham is the most suburban city in Britain. It expanded so fast, from the late eighteenth century, that it became the second largest city after London. The cheapest ornaments and jewellery were made here (hence the sneer-word 'brummagem') and, for almost a century, a large proportion of Britain's cars. With demography, you always have to talk definitions. Birmingham's great rival for the title of Second City is the city of Manchester. But 'Manchester' is, technically, a narrow strip in the middle of the Greater Manchester conurbation. Even the other bank of Manchester's river, the Irwell, is run by a separate local authority, the city of Salford. The burghers of Birmingham played a different boundary game. As the city grew, they kept extending its legal limits. Within these, it embarked on enormous municipal suburban estates. The writer Lynsey Hanley, who was born in one of them, The Wood, powerfully chronicled the grimmer side in her polemical memoir *Estates: An Intimate History*. But Birmingham also played host to wide swathes of comfortable, privately owned houses. Both varieties of new home began life closer to the city centre, in the Cadbury model village of Bournville and in the model suburb of Edgbaston.

Both these phenomena came to the city of Birmingham through the workings of land ownership: Bournville through the Cadbury purchase of land near their new out-of-town chocolate factory; Edgbaston through the private enterprise of the Anstruther-Gough-Calthorpe family. Both are unique, in their separate ways. Birmingham has always liked novelty, and both ideas were hot off the press.

Bournville predates all the various garden cities and New Towns. On Merseyside, the soap maker William Lever (Lord Leverhulme) built Port Sunlight as a model village for his own workers. But this remained a company town, a glorified set of tied cottages. If you stopped working for him, you lost your home. Bournville was always more liberal. To get a house, it helped if you worked for Cadbury. But you were then given tenure, regardless.

At first, beginning in 1894, George Cadbury had sold the houses on long leases. But he soon realised that his workpeople couldn't afford this. He set up the Bournville trust, independent of the factory. Tenants paid an economic rent. Light and air were at the heart of Cadbury's concept of development. This meant wide roads and large gardens. Each house only covered a quarter of its site. When new occupants arrived, they found that the gardens had already been

Soap king William Lever began building Port Sunlight on the Wirral, Merseyside, from the 1890s as good homes for his workpeople. 'Sunlight' was his patent soap. Every bar was stamped with the product name: a novel publicity idea. Lever rose to fame, fortune and a viscountcy.

laid out, and fruit trees planted. As in the garden cities and the early council estates, the thought was that, in hard times, you could grow your own food. There was a school, a village institute (named after Ruskin) and a Quaker meeting house. It is all very pretty, though without a single gleam of great architecture. To echo William Morris, it was known to be useful – a fact which has a beauty of its own.

The one-time suburban village is now enclosed by even newer suburbs. Most visitors, I noticed, seemed to go past Bournville now, on their way to Cadbury's 'Chocolate World.' Cadbury's were prevented by health regulations from continuing to show people round the actual works. They then had the clever idea of persuading them to pay for going round what is, in effect, a Cadbury marketing display. Even the name Bournville had been clever marketing. It was applied to the chocolate before it was given to the village. French chocolate was highly regarded. 'Bournville' was brummagem French. The firm's cheap chocolate was sold everywhere. It was cheap because it had so little cocoa butter in it. In due course, the European Union had to come up with a new euphemism ('family milk chocolate') to allow it to be sold on the same shelves as the pukka Swiss, Belgian or French versions.

Edgbaston was built for a different class of people. The first issue of *Edgbastonia* magazine in 1881 stated: 'Unquestionably the most important suburb of Birmingham, the favourite place of residence for the professional men and traders of the busy town which it adjoins.' This is still more or less true; the professionals now include the academics of the University of Birmingham and the doctors of the immense Queen Elizabeth teaching hospital, both of which are in Edgbaston.

At the charming Botanical Gardens, Edgbaston, the young mothers came with their smart buggies, ready to inspect the banana trees and watch the darting parakeets. The shop sold garden kneelers, wooden jigsaws and little floral piggy banks, which looked highly English but were, when I looked under a piglet's belly, made in China.

The shop also sold greetings-card versions of the 'Social Stereotypes' series, which was running every Saturday in the *Telegraph Magazine*. I wondered who exactly, and on what occasion, would send the card of 'The Mistress' (always waiting, we were told, over a bottle of Sancerre for that delayed phone call, while confiding in her gay friend, Clive). Or 'The Cleaning Lady', whom apparently her boss thinks of as 'Mrs Danvers with Pledge', but is reconciled to putting up with, pending some Latvian alternative.

Just across the road from central Birmingham, Edgbaston is a kind of red-brick heaven. As I emerged from a grotty underpass, it announced itself immediately: a small clothes shop selling Christian Lacroix dresses. This is a suburb that has never gone down in the world. It has benefited from clever private control. The Anstruther-Gough-Calthorpe family may now sell, rather than lease. But freehold comes with a wodge of restrictions: no tree felling; mend your fences and windows – or the estate will do it for you, and charge. Along the Chad valley (more of a furrow, really), the neo-Tudor semis are as neat as toy houses, the camellias pruned, the hedges clipped.

Edgbaston is, among other things, Birmingham's conscience: the conscience of the rich. The university, which nestles within Edgbaston, is probably best known to many people as David Lodge's University of Rummidge, the setting for his campus novels. In *Nice Work*, on an adult job-experience scheme, Dr Robyn Penrose commutes from the campus to test out her semiotic theories (and much else) on the managing director of J. Pringle & Sons, Casting and General Engineering. Edgbaston is also home to the King Edward VI grammar schools, ex-direct grant but driven back into the private sector by a 1970s Labour government. And to Warwickshire cricket ground.

The Chad Square estate agent told me he sold to professionals: solicitors, architects, accountants. 'And also to members of the ethnic community. They're often in the clothing trade. One man we just sold to – his grandfather came over and started by selling dishcloths.' As if on cue, a seven-year-old Indian boy came in for a free newspaper, and took it out to his mother in a Mercedes. 'I always say, "Welcome to Ambridge",' the estate agent said. 'Everyone knows everyone else's business. What they don't know, they make up.'

Birmingham Botanical Gardens, one of the delights of Edgbaston. This suburb embedded within the heart of the city is home, also, to the University of Birmingham (David Lodge's 'fictional' University of Rummidge), the teaching hospital, an excellent art gallery and Warwickshire county cricket ground. Edgbaston sees itself as the city's conscience.

Signs in the subtropical glasshouse at Birmingham Botanical Gardens

Chad Square had nine shops. From left to right: dry cleaning, wine, artificial flowers, dresses, a restaurant (sparkling white linen, mushrooms on bruschetta, corn-fed chicken breast, sticky toffee pudding), estate agent, tailor, newsagent, pizza house. It is the sort of shopping parade, built in the 1960s, which in most places are down at heel. Not in Edgbaston.

The tailor, Ahmet Yusuf, was a cheerful man, whose greatest anxiety was robberies. 'Motorways have been bad for us. The thieves come in from Liverpool, Manchester.' After a robbery with gun, 'they found the car burnt out somewhere up north'. Yusuf arrived from Cyprus in 1954. He had a needle in one lapel and a Rotary Club buttonhole in the other. In the back of the shop, the staff sat and sewed among the hanging suits. A newspaper was open at the headline: 'Germany Shuts Door to the Turks'. 'Birmingham was a dark city, when I came,' he said. 'You put on a clean collar – it was dirty by the time you crossed town. It's changed lovely.' Suburban Edgbaston has stayed detergent-clean all the time.

It wasn't entirely a joke when James Bartholomew, a *Daily Telegraph* writer, published a book called *Yew and Non-Yew*, in horticultural homage to Nancy Mitford's *U and Non-U*. After her exploration of verbal snobbery, he was exploring garden snobbery. He subtitled his book: *Gardening for Horticultural Climbers*. He mapped the constant suburban tussle between trying to keep up with the experts (and with the aristos, as displayed for public consumption in *Hudson's Historic Houses & Gardens* guide), and just doing what you wanted. One chapter was headed 'The dahlia question': 'The Non-Yew gardener thinks they are a wonderful triumph of man and nature combined. The Yew gardener thinks they are a revolting perversion.'

Like everything else, horticultural taste takes surprising turns (see James Laver, above). In a way, that is the point of it. How else do you keep ahead of the herd? The trend-setting garden writer Christopher Lloyd threw horticultural fashionistas into a tremendous tizz when he ripped out his highly 'Yew' rose garden, with all the correct varieties of old rose, and included dahlias in the re-planting. In suburbia, decisions about the hedge matter most: not merely privacy, but the right sort of privacy. This is the garden as seen by the public and the neighbours. Here is a selection from Bartholomew's hedge listings:

Yew: Yew (of course), beech, holly, hornbeam, tapestry (mixture of any of these).
Non-Yew: *leylandii* cypress (green or golden), spotted laurel.

You can see that it is an endless struggle – if you care about such things – to stay on the right side of the horticultural divide. Lloyd brought dahlias back into bourgeois respectability. There were limits. He rather liked conifers, but he also wrote of 'the thuggish habits of the Leyland cypress'. I saw from the *Daily Telegraph*'s gardening section, as I wrote this, that Bob Brown, 'one of the great British nurserymen', was due to launch a Foliage Society, a club 'that celebrates and promotes the beauty of the leaf'. It was to be launched at the Royal Horticultural Society annual show at Malvern. Whatever the glories of the yew tree are – darkness, ancientness, poisonousness? – foliage isn't one of them. No matter. Nothing could sound more Yew than Mr Brown's bright new idea.

But would his trees and hedges attract the right sort of birds? The environment quango, Natural England, had reported that wild birds were fleeing intensely farmed lowland fields and taking refuge in suburban gardens. Some butterfly species now lived wholly in the suburbs. This gave new openings for social competition. Blue tits were seen as 'amusing' but really rather commonplace. All garden centres started to offer specialist seed packets, aimed at fancier visitors. Among these packets, the great newcomer was niger seed – now often re-spelled 'nijer' seed, to make sure that no one unwittingly pronounced it 'nigger'. Extracted from an Ethiopian thistle, it was flown into Stansted airport, and much loved (it said on the packet) by greenfinches. Not that it always worked. One disappointed suburban gardener wrote to the newspaper to say that he had seen no greenfinches so far – but he had a wonderful crop of thistles.

Looking out over our own garden, I see that we have both magnolia (top tree in the Yew stakes) and golden robinia (almost as Non-Yew as flowering cherry or eucalyptus). In suburban Walthamstow, fortunately for everyone's peace of mind, the anxious planting of hedges and trees, and the assiduous wooing of greenfinches, is not at all what allotments are about.

9. THE LAND FETISH

Few of the postwar New Towns can be counted as a great success. You can check this out at Stevenage, in Hertfordshire. This was the first of them, launched on 11 November 1946, three months after the passage of the New Towns Act. It met with much local opposition, and was nicknamed Silkingrad, after the then Housing Minister, Lewis Silkin. The New Town has some surprising sides to it. For example, it is the headquarters of the Wine Society, a rare example in Britain of a true cooperative firm, wholly owned by its members. It is a rather fancy example: not exactly the workers' control of radical dreams. The Wine Society moved out of London in 1965 to save money on rent and to gain a better space for storage. Otherwise, it had looked like folding. Now it flourishes.

A major flaw marred Stevenage. It was the same snag faced by its forerunner garden cities and garden suburbs: Letchworth, Welwyn, Hemel Hempstead, all in Hertfordshire; Bedford Park, Hampstead Garden Suburb, in west and north London; and Wythenshawe in southern Manchester. They all left decisions about a true centre till last. In organic urban or suburban growth, the centre comes first, or at least very early on. In contrast, the impetus with all these ventures was always to get more houses built; usually with high ideals, never fulfilled for long, about creating 'mixed' communities. The upshot was towns and suburbs with a curious hole in the middle. At Stevenage, after many years of belated effort, the town centre still struck me as being as grubby and unappealing as Basildon's. The much-photographed 1950s clock tower, adorned with a portrait of Silkin, was surrounded by a protective wire fence. Primark was much the busiest store. A hotdog stand had a small, patient queue. A blind man, who looked about thirty, was begging at the corner. A shabby window display behind him announced, unconvincingly, a proposed regeneration scheme. A concrete walkway led through a run-down leisure centre to the railway station. The Gordon Craig Theatre advertised 'Allo 'Allo, based on the long-gone TV farce, but now 'live on stage'. 'Comedy from the Golden Age', *The Times* had apparently said. Craig (1869–1966), the out-of-wedlock son of the actress Ellen Terry, was born in Railway Street, in old Stevenage. He became the acclaimed, visionary pioneer of modern theatre design and direction. For this?

Opposite: Barratt builds its own ideal of family happiness. Houses on the site of a former print works, Paulton, Somerset, an exurb of Bath and Bristol.

Stevenage New Town centre: a planner's dream. It looked better when new (1958).

To many visitors' surprise, there is still an old Stevenage, the former village centre. It is now, so to speak, a suburb of the New Town. It still has the attractiveness of an older rural Hertfordshire market town: wine bars, smart pubs, the decorous blue hoarding of a prep school. Or, more precisely, old Stevenage has the attractiveness of London's exurbia.

In the beginning, the Stevenage economy was rescued from the doldrums by firms gifted with defence contracts, British Aerospace especially. As the economic historian Sydney Checkland pointed out in *The Upas Tree*, his sharp-eyed study of the decline of Glasgow as an industrial city, politically motivated defence contracts are a short-term wonder and a long-term disaster. Glasgow's core trades of shipbuilding and heavy engineering were propped up by naval and military orders, which, as the threat of world war receded, were cut back or dropped. In Javanese fables, the upas tree exuded a lethal poison, killing off everything for miles around. The history of defence contracts shows that what politics allots, politics can take away. Such contracts are not operating in a genuine market. They bring shed-loads of money but, from the experience of Glasgow, Checkland argued that the money comes too easily. It deters the creation of new initiatives, new inventions, new markets. The firms are operating at someone's, or some government's, whim. Stevenage has, so far, had a better short-term inheritance than Glasgow. The New Town's top employers are MBDA (missiles), Astrium (spacecraft launchers) and GlaxoSmithKline (pharmaceuticals). It is less certain what the long-term answer will be. Already, many Stevenagers commute, to London or elsewhere.

The truth that it is hard to create communities from scratch seems to require rediscovery in every generation. One reason why suburbs work better than new settlements, set down in the middle of nowhere, is that they are building on what was there before. Quantity changes quality (as Karl Marx argued). But it doesn't change it completely. The governments led by Tony Blair and Gordon Brown thought they could end a housing shortage, which they themselves had allowed to fester, by endorsing what they called 'eco-towns'. The planned ten would have between 5,000 and 15,000 houses on each site. Most would be not much more than New Villages, several of them built on old military bases, which the government had been finding it hard to sell off. There was no obvious back-up of educational or health services. There would be nothing ecological about the amount of petrol it would require to live in them, and commute for every known need.

The eco-towns scheme was one outcome of what Peter Hall has called 'the land fetish', the passion to preserve all land at all costs, irrespective of its actual use. The hope, perhaps, was that the smallness of the planned eco-towns would help them to escape criticism. It didn't. The *Daily Telegraph*, under the headline 'Middle England rises against plans for 200,000 eco-homes', was soon chronicling the rising tide of protest signatures, including 'the likes of the Oscar winning actress Dame Judi Dench and the parents of the former tennis player Tim Henman'. And these objectors were not alone. It would, surely, have been much better to build new suburbs or to expand exurbs: picking up the baton of success, rather than start the race with a heavy handicap. Such a plan would have produced the cry, which is the

The high street of old Stevenage – which just happened (with a little help from conservationists).

in Cranford branch library. On the shelves, Hounslow social services' guides were printed in Gujarati, Punjabi and Polish. At the bus stop outside, a young Asian woman in her smart check-in uniform waited for the No. 105, which ran into Heathrow bus station. The bus arrived full of other Asian airport staff, from its previous stop in Southall, that wondrous India-in-London suburb.

To be in Cranford, Middlesex, was like watching a hive of bees. At the main roundabout, two of the four exits directed you to different terminals. All the local businesses seemed to have some Heathrow connection. Some of them were huge, like Irish Cargo Express Forwarding or the Western International Market (air-freighted fruit and veg). But then there were little firms like Stor-A-Car (24 hour off-airport parking), Electronic Flight Specialists and even the Airport Motor Radiator Co.

I stood by the road, next to the destroyed countryside (a caravan in a field with horses, link fencing everywhere, dumped fridges) and watched the cars and lorries: DHL, Ryder Truck Rental, CCF Couriers, Global Transport Services, Leggett Freightways, United Couriers, Securicor Omega Express, WVC Self-Drive Hire. It was an astonishing display of commercial mobility. No one, I thought, would ever put this genie back into its bottle.

Cranford is not beautiful. But the old docks of London and other cities were like this once: an unstructured, unending hubbub, on a permanent building or rebuilding site. In the distance I could see the enormous hangars and cargo sheds of the airport. The most characteristic building of the early twenty-first century is a warehouse – usually at a town edge or at a motorway junction where it is obviously going to become the node for many more. Paradoxically, the unlovely suburb of Cranford, Middlesex, slots neatly into William Morris's set of criteria. It may not be beautiful (not everything can be), but it is unquestionably useful. A huge yellow roadside sign announced: 'Himalaya Carpets. 2,000 designs in stock. Low, low, low prices.'

Those who oppose suburbia usually have highly doctrinaire views about how other people should live. This helps them to hold down the building of new homes. Between the two world wars, in spite of the much derided growth of suburbia, many couples had to live as 'concealed' families – 'part of someone else's household . . . the housing stock was much smaller than the number of households'. The words are by Alan Holmans, former chief housing economist at the Department of the Environment and later a research fellow at Cambridge,

A plane flies out of Heathrow, over a Hounslow rooftop: the exact economic equivalent of ships leaving or entering the Wapping or Isle of Dogs docks, before they collapsed.

in his contribution to the Town and Country Planning Association report, *The People – Where Will They Go?* Few people want to live like that now or did, even then. Nor can anyone be forced to who has the money, or the credit rating, to gain access to the housing market. Holmans again: 'Under ordinary law (as distinct from wartime powers) there is no means of applying judgments about what accommodation is "really needed" to people who can afford market prices or rents. Only those who depend on subsidy are within reach of such policies.' It's the rich that get the pleasure, and the poor that get told what to do.

In London, under pressure from Ken Livingstone's 2000–8 mayoralty, more and more flats were built. The will-o'-the-wisp hope was that all the extra population could be rammed into the existing Greater London Authority boundaries. Did the pursuit of votes influence this? Such an ambition would be nothing new. In defence of the house building programmes of the old London County Council (abolished in 1965), the LCC's Labour Party political boss Herbert Morrison is said to have boasted: 'We'll build the Tories out of London.' The remark is possibly apocryphal. His biographers found no written evidence of it. To find it might require reading every local newspaper report of every Morrison speech. But it neatly sums up Morrison's sentiments.

The recent campaign to build either flats or quite small houses was especially strong in the 'Thames Gateway' (formerly known, less glamorously, as the East Thames Corridor). This comprises thousands of acres of often unappealing land east and south-east of the capital. The ownership of flats built in such places became a strange phenomenon. Many were bought by buy-to-let speculators. Some became the home base of people spending much of their time abroad. Some were the London base for people with second homes in the countryside. Students, or their parents, acquired others. Flats and houses in Thames Gateway were almost always two-bedroom, which is less than most families these days would like to have. In other words, they were starter homes for young couples or for dedicated singletons, possibly gay. None of these occupants were likely to bring about the usual kind of community. For this, as in the past, families with children are at the heart of the matter.

The 1996 planning association study found that 'As a general rule, the demand for housing and readily available sites do not coincide geographically. Demand falls largely on suburban or exurban locations.' The authors' judgment was that the 'prospects for the development of urban brownfield sites are poor'.

The reasons were: contamination, poor access, weak demand, high costs. There was also the difficulty of selling and, even harder, re-selling properties built in such locations, especially if they were also high-rise or high-density. The authors' conclusion was: 'Most analysis suggests that urban decentralisation will continue.' And if you don't build the houses, the government's own Review of Housing Supply concluded in 2004 that, in Britain: 'Higher demand . . . tends to be translated into higher house prices rather than increased output of houses . . . fuelling concerns about affordability, with unwelcome effects on individuals and the economy.' For non-home owners, the review correctly forecast, 'the distribution of wealth will become increasingly unequal'.

For a while, banks like Northern Rock persuaded newer, poorer customers that they could redress the inequality by taking out a mortgage they couldn't really afford on a house that wasn't really worth it. In 2008, such policies in both America and Britain brought about the 'sub-prime' credit crisis. More and more buyers defaulted. The banks engaged in this dubious business ran out of cash. The banks' chief executives took early retirement, clutching their golden goodbyes. The mortgagers had their homes repossessed. They went back to their social housing or mobile home parks. House prices sank, but they didn't benefit. The inequalities were put back in place.

The house-price story shouldn't be very surprising. If you restrict supply, and demand is still strong, the cost will go up. In and around London, the political power of 'what we have, we hold' made it very difficult to change this. Yet all projections showed that little green, or greenish, land would have to be sacrificed to meet present or future demand. In the south-east, the government's review reported, about 60 per cent of the land was out of bounds (as green belt, or as a designated or protected area). About 11 per cent was built on. Leaving aside the case for reshaping the boundaries of the green belt – which has already happened, slightly – the review reckoned that only about 1.5 per cent of the remaining 29 per cent of land would be needed for new houses. That is, less than 0.5 per cent of all land in the south-east.

One environmentalist contributor to the 1996 report noted that 'all long-range forecasts hitherto have been wrong. No prediction of any human activity can be immune to the ability of those humans to decide to act differently.' He was right. In particular, all demographic forecasts that are based on guesses about future birth rates are always inaccurate. The crucial decisions are taken by two people on their

Suburbia can't be understood without understanding the (sometimes fanatical) love of gardens. Opposite, above left: Camouflaged wheelie bin, Hampstead Garden Suburb. Above right: Topiary arch, Shepherds Bush, west London. Bottom left: Leylandii, Heaton Moor, Stockport. Bottom right: Monkey puzzle tree, Bingley. This page, above left : Conifers, Craigleith, Edinburgh. Below left: Dollis Hill spirals, north west London. Below right: Pampas grass, Camberley, Surrey.

his classic book, *The Making of the English Landscape*, W.G. Hoskins emphasises that this landscape is an almost wholly human invention. After centuries of agriculture, industry and mineral extraction, nothing 'natural' is left. In recent years, the re-sculpted minelands are one of the biggest human additions to the landscape of Britain since parliamentary enclosure threw across it the network of hedges and dry-stone walling which is often defended as if it has always been there. To find a greener England: go north.

For a century or so, the industrial revolution shifted the economic and social balance within Britain. Before then, the south had always been preponderant. It is often not realised that, even in the heyday of the north, London, with its own specialisms (often related to the docks), had more workers in industrial jobs than any other city in Britain. The signs that the balance was shifting back became evident in the early twentieth century. The most symbolic signs were when Cunard switched the route of its transatlantic liners from Liverpool to Southampton in 1919; when Marks & Spencer transferred its headquarters offices from Manchester to the City of London in 1924; and when Ford moved its car works from Trafford to Dagenham in 1931. There is no sign yet that the balance will swing away again from the south.

They have been very busy changing the landscape in County Durham, south Yorkshire and Nottinghamshire. The old minefields have almost sunk back into countryside. As I went around, I saw everywhere the oddly perfect, rather flattened hills. They had no stone walls or fencing on them. Often the only soil cover, still, was grass. But the landscape designers have moved on to quick-growing trees, like silver birch, which will give shelter to slower growths.

Until the Aberfan disaster of 1966, in which 144 died (116 of them children), old spoil heaps were mostly left standing: bleak and sulphurous. Since then, they have been lowered, and sculpted into a simulacrum of nature. As more and more coal mines closed down, this process speeded up. The earth-movers were an Old Testament plague of locusts in reverse: making the land turn green again. Just south of Worksop, in Nottinghamshire, I saw the work still in progress. A cluster of new roads and roundabouts was hedged about with earthworks: a kind of punitive beautification. The bare soil was being smoothed over in whorls, as if an amateur plasterer had been let loose on it. In the early twenty-first century, it is astonishing in Britain to see an active pit (though open-cast quietly flourishes). It is like a glimpse of a megasaurus.

South Wales and Scotland have shared this history of a collapsed industry, and a vanishing way of life. Even so, northern England is a special case. I found it extraordinarily moving to take a train through County Durham and realise that not a single pit was left. Nor in Northumberland either. To children now in school, 'coals to Newcastle' in a classroom text will have to be footnoted, like 'hoist with their own petard' or 'blotted his escutcheon'. It is a fossilised metaphor, a fly in the amber of language. I stood one morning outside the pit gates at Easington Colliery, among men struggling to keep tears back as they watched the winding gear demolished. All that is over.

The coal pits have gone the same way as the lead mines of the Lake District and the tin mines of Cornwall. How long before we get a Minelands National Park? In Yorkshire, in an old pit, there is already a National Mining Museum. Ken Loach's film *Kes* (1969) was a portrait of the sour realities of mine work in progress. The later film *Brassed Off* (1996), also set in the Yorkshire coalfield, was a cornet-blast of farewell to what had gone. Perhaps both will be on permanent loop in a new Minelands National Park's visitor centre. An actor, down on his luck, will give readings from Lawrence's *The White Peacock*.

In south Yorkshire, English Heritage restored Brodsworth Hall, a mansion outside Doncaster. I went along to see it re-opened. The main restoration problem was that the mine the family had dug, in order to keep themselves in racehorses and yachts, ran under the house. Subsidence made it tilt. Gutters began to slope the wrong way. The rain ran down inside, onto the expensively tooled wallpaper and the bare-bosomed, bare-bottomed nymphs. The fine trees the family planted, to screen out the pithead and the spoil heaps of their mine, were still standing, I noticed. But beyond the trees lay only another gentle, artificial hill. There was no 'squire' now, and no miners either.

It was once said that the coal miner was 'a Turk at home' because he was 'a slave at work'. The social change has been painful. In a County Durham shopping centre, I saw fit young men pushing baby buggies in the middle of the day, when they would previously have been down the pit. Neither they nor their wives looked very happy about it.

Britain is an 'island made mainly of coal', the radical Labour leader Aneurin Bevan told the party faithful in 1945. He foresaw no change. This was another future that didn't turn out as expected. The good old songs need rewriting. Yes, we have re-built Jerusalem: as proof you can see a new green hill, not far away.

10. THE NEW JERUSALEM

Milton Keynes was intended as a New Jerusalem. It is now, often, a joke (as Slough was to Betjeman in his famous, or notorious, poem). In fact it was an attempt, unique in Britain, to follow in London's path and recreate the idea of the city-as-suburb. Of the various towns created under the New Towns Act, it is far and away the most successful, partly because it is so big. In spite of the amount of land it occupies, even the most ardent eco-warrior should applaud it. And not just because of its 22 million trees. The great majority of Milton Keynes's employed inhabitants have jobs within its boundaries, and can even go to them on a special network of cycle-ways, if they choose to.

There is something Dutch about Milton Keynes. The flat north Buckinghamshire plain is kept dry by little storage channels and some rather beautiful storage lakes. To people who have never been there, or who just drive through, it is best known as a city for cars. But when you get out of your car, you are most conscious of the interlinked bike lanes crisscrossing from neighbourhood to neighbourhood, between and under the rectilinear grid of main roads (a Mondrian made tarmac). The townscape has the cool rationalism of the men who sat down and decided that the Zuider Zee should be turned into *terra firma*.

A cyclist in a flat, drained landscape, which is divided mathematically into squares: this would be a poster image of Holland, but also of Milton Keynes. It was the culmination, the high point, of the New Towns Act. Designated twenty years after Stevenage, it too was very much a Labour Party creation. The then Housing Minister Anthony Greenwood, who christened it, was delighted to find that the town's site included a tiny village with such a significant double-barrelled name: one poet plus one economist. The naming was Greenwood's only public achievement. He once said: 'I may be no good as a minister, but I'm very good in bed.'

Even now, an aura of Harold Wilson's Labour administrations lingers. The Open University is here, which Wilson later said was his proudest achievement. The campus has a Wilson Building and a Jenny Lee Library, named after, and opened by, his Arts Minister. Some of the ideas for the Open University came from the sociologist and educationist Michael Young (including, he always

Opposite: This Indian restaurant, in central Milton Keynes, claims to be the largest purpose-built example 'in Europe – maybe the world'.

maintained, the suggestion that it should be sited in Milton Keynes). There is a Michael Young Building. So the trio of patron saints are all properly remembered. This first British open-access university would never have happened without Jenny Lee's huge enthusiasm and drive, and her great personal influence on Wilson. This was always a subject of some mystery and gossip.

The party connection continued. The first head of the New Town's development corporation was Lord (Jock) Campbell of Eskan, multi-millionaire socialist and chairman of a left-wing weekly magazine, the *New Statesman*. In the middle of town, Campbell Park commemorates him. A plaque under a tall yew hedge says: *Si monumentum requiris, circumspice*. The original of that inscription is on Christopher Wren's tomb in St Paul's. Milton Keynes sings from a different hymnbook: no autocratic baroque beauty here. But it is proud of being such a stunning success, socially and economically. Use before beauty, again. The enthronement of suburbia. It is also a place that people who don't live there love to hate. In this, there is a mingled brew of snobbery and jealousy.

In the nineteenth century, Britain's fastest-growing town was Merthyr Tydfil in south Wales. In the late twentieth and early twenty-first centuries it has been Milton Keynes. The contrast is comforting. Perhaps the Victorians were right, and there is such a thing as Progress with a capital P, after all. Here speaks a visitor to Merthyr in its grubby, coal-and-iron heyday: 'We went out to a height above the town, whence we had a view of five or six of these [iron] works where fires are constantly kept up by night as well as by day. One might imagine oneself in the land of the Cyclops.' And this is how the iron-workers lived: 'The space between these houses is generally very limited; an open stinking and nearly stagnant gutter, into which the house refuse is, as usual, flung, moves slowly before the doors. It is a labyrinth of miserable tenements and filth, filled with people . . .'

Milton Keynes, the *über*-suburb, is how a good proportion of the British people would now like to live, given the chance. It is a town of (on the whole) the young. Those who prosper here are, above all, people who would once have been called the lower middle class: not lawyers or riveters, but technicians and office workers. Hence some of the snobbery. But this happens to be the characteristic class of contemporary Britain. And walking around, you do feel that people here live like equals, in spite of economic disparities. It is the psychology of Utrecht or Yonkers: all very un-English.

'MK', as its citizens always call it, in conscious imitation of LA for Los Angeles, is like an advertisement for itself. As soon as I turned into it from the M1, I saw the globular lights that are the place's trademark. And everywhere there were trees: no houses immediately visible. In the far distance, on a slight rise, were a cluster of white buildings, with a single dome: the new Jerusalem itself. But not quite a city on a hill: MK is a horizontal city. After a while, I began to suffer from a form of sensory deprivation: a vacuum of verticals. The dome is the central church – omni-denominational, inevitably, including the RCs (but not Muslims, who have a minaret-free mosque well away from the centre). The church's dome is suitably low. Elsewhere in the Midlands plain, they usually go in for a tall, heavenward spire. Milton Keynes keeps its head down.

On this cold wet day, the wind whipped across the town. Trying to get a grip on the geography, I kept in my mind's eye that gridiron layout of north–south and east–west roads. Commonplace in America, such a grid in Britain is only usual in the urbane layouts of the landowners who prospered under

Milton Keynes always advertises itself as the city of trees. Here is a metal sculpture of this trademark, entitled 'A Tree of Life'. In the background, the Xscape indoor ski run.

the Houses of Orange and Hanover: Marylebone in London, the New Town in Edinburgh. In Milton Keynes, some confusion has been caused by the road engineers. In the prevailing fashion of the 1960s and 1970s, they insisted on putting a hefty roundabout at each intersection. This makes it much harder to tell your north from your west, and your east from your south, and much easier (as I found) to get lost.

The intellectual founding father of MK was Melvin Webber, an amiable American professor from Berkeley, California. He was an adviser on the New Town's original plan, in 1967. To Webber, looking at California, the future was a rationalised Los Angeles. In the city-as-suburb, he argued, people would be brought together into communities, not by propinquity, but by shared interests. The thought first struck him when he noticed how much time Californians spent on the telephone, even in the days of landlines. On this interpretation, the best urban design would be a set of empty containers into which an infinite number of options could be poured. It was a recipe for a beneficent anarchy. Webber, teasingly, called his vision the 'non-place urban realm'. This was the absolute opposite of the previous garden city or garden suburb ideal. There, the planners had a very clear idea of what the people were supposed to do, and when (even if things didn't always turn out like that). Letchworth, Welwyn, Stevenage, Cumbernauld: all were corsets. Milton Keynes was to be Lycra-stretch.

And it is. To have created a working town of more than 222,000 people at the last count – that is, bigger than Oxford and getting close to Nottingham – in less than half a century is an extraordinary achievement. The town plans to house well over 315,000 by the 2031 census; 'as big as Cardiff', the council boasts (bigger, by my reckoning, and a good deal pleasanter). Before then, it will surely have achieved its longed-for formal designation of 'city'. (In one selection round, it lost out to Sunderland, which, that way at least, caught up with its old rival, Newcastle.) In this chapter, let me grant MK citydom from here in on. 'Of

Like much of suburbia, Milton Keynes loves horses – and shop-front puns ('tack' means saddles and bridles).

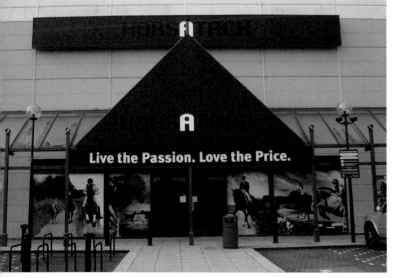

course,' the development corporation's first general manager, Fred Roche, told me as we sat one day in the Post House hotel, just down from Midsummer Boulevard, 'you would have to be even more bloody fools than we were to make a failure of a New Town put down between Birmingham and London, on the direct motorway and rail links. Milton Keynes is about Arcadia – planned suburbia – but the economic base has been created. There have been tremendous shifts – employment, leisure, home ownership, aspirations – yet Milton Keynes has adapted to all of them.'

In launching MK, the corporation was determined not to fall into the garden city trap of leaving some kind of city centre till last. The upshot was the very model of an American-style Edge City. In 1973–9, the first mall in Britain was built, 700 yards long, in the middle of the north Buckinghamshire countryside. It was always seen as a place people would come miles to shop in, not just the inhabitants of Milton Keynes. Close around the mall, Edge-City-wise, have grown hunks of office space, more shops, entertainment zones, hotels. There are some flats, but beyond them lie the houses, acre after acre. Each grid square is a neighbourhood of its own, sometimes with an old, pretty church from some pre-existing village. Together with the raw commercial vigour of the city centre, these churches have sucked the lifeblood out of the Church of Christ the Cornerstone, stranded between the mall and a row of offices. In spite of its dome, the church looks cheap and dull, even more so inside than out. The worship space is like a Job Centre waiting room. A stall sells fridge magnets with sad little messages: 'Grant me patience, Lord, but hurry.' The magnets were made in Stoke-on-Trent by Brontë Products. Emily, Charlotte and Anne's father, the Reverend Patrick Brontë, would not be amused. More characteristic of Milton Keynes's spiritual side, I thought, was the energetic 'Race for Life' they were organising in Campbell Park, to raise money for cancer research. Territorials were laying out the route. Two policemen in yellow Day-Glo jackets rode up on bikes – when did I last see a copper on a bike? – to see how things were going.

This is a city of small firms, or at least small premises. At first the railways and the Open University were the largest employers. The Open U still is, with 5,000 staff. Small Victorian towns like Wolverton or Bletchley were railway settlements before they became re-invented as districts of Milton Keynes, and rail work isn't what it was. The average MK firm employs fewer than twenty staff. But averages are, as always, a bit misleading. Foreign firms came to MK like flies to a honey pot: Coca-Cola and Volkswagen, for example – but for bottling, back office work and spares, not usually for manufacture. The biggest employers include the offices of the Abbey/Santander bank (1,700 staff, but for how much longer?) and Argos (1,100). From a gigantic warehouse – its size cleverly disguised by being painted in shades of blue, which merge into the sky – John Lewis distributes to all its stores in Britain. The Institute of Chartered Accountants in England and Wales has its head office here, which seems wise as Milton Keynes claims to have 169 accountancy firms.

Except at the dwindling rail works, trades unions found it hard to organise. So, as well as space for new premises, MK often meant a lower wage bill. Today, as I drove into a hedgerowed car park, the Open University campus looked like the nearest thing in MK to an old-style factory: a diploma manufacturer's mill. Walton Hall, where the OU began, was now a tiny island of Georgian architecture among high, glass-sided blocks. In essence, the OU is a vast publishing business. That morning all the Renaults, Skodas and Hondas were checking in. Cyclists came along the special bikeways, past a willow-lined brook.

The first houses at Milton Keynes were all publicly owned, and to rent. The city has since gone private. Some of the earlier buildings now look pretty terrible. In its early, higher-minded years, MK welcomed in London's ill-housed and under-skilled. Some of these families are still here. As at Basildon a fine film of social differentiation has settled on Milton Keynes, like dust. In the Beanhill district, the young Norman Foster built rows and rows of metal-sided boxes, reminiscent of a South African township. (They don't feature very prominently in his published work.) The boxes have since had pitched, tiled roofs put on them. As I went round, I recognised Beanhill as echoing one side of California, at least when the sun came out: the under-side. Cardboard and plastic packaging was piled in front gardens. A man was oiling a tractor. A converted blue and white bus had curtains at all the windows, a crowd of fluffy toys in front, and plenty of England stickers. All the cars, parked with two wheels on the pavements, were old and often battered. There were children everywhere, with their parents, on their bikes, or just sitting. A little black boy stared at me, in friendly curiosity, as I wandered around.

The children were the attractive aspect of Beanhill. You seldom see children playing out on streets anywhere in Britain. One exception is the Muslim backstreets of Bradford. A snapshot of Beanhill would rival those in Colin

Ward's *The Child in the City* – perhaps his most original book – where he argued forcefully that the best way to judge the liveability of a city was by the way a child would experience it. Ward's cover picture is of summertime Manchester children, against the backdrop of a cotton factory, playing in a sluice of the Rochdale canal. Successors to Iona and Peter Opie could research in Beanhill an update of their classic *Children's Games in Street and Playground*. Near by, at Netherfield, from the same era, industrialised three-storey rows looked grimmer than a refugee camp. The prefabricated neighbourhood shopping centre had men with not enough to do except crowd into the built-in pub, and mothers with more children than they knew how to cope with. In a shop window were the characteristic for-sale-or-rent postcards of the poor: 'One laddy's bike'; 'Furnished room. Working person preferred'; 'Rottweiler puppies'. I would bet it is hard to get a good job offer if the employer discovers that you come from Beanhill or Netherfield.

Elsewhere, you are astonished by the sheer profusion of housing, in every variety from standard spec, through a sprinkling of now rather dated Post-Modern, and on to glassy neo-Modernist, with its assorted homages to Mies van der Rohe, Alvar Aalto and Frank Lloyd Wright. An architectural pot-pourri. Here you come across a classical obelisk; there, a long, ochre-brick crescent. MK has elbowed its way out of any original planster constraints. Fabianism gave way to Thatcherism.

At Thirlby Lane, in the Shenley Church End neighbourhood, Bovis the builders decided to try to tempt some of the bosses of MK firms to buy homes within this city of suburbs, instead of in the villages of north Buckinghamshire or in the small market town of Buckingham itself. New, high, reed-thatched 'farmhouses' were designed. The centrepiece was a repro manor house. Some were half-timbered. One had a wych-gate. All around here, two garages seemed to be the absolute minimum. I talked to a joiner working at one house. He lived in Milton Keynes, and loved it. He was brought up in 'Old Welwyn', he said, as opposed to Ebenezer Howard's garden city. Suburbia lives or dies by such tiny, but important, shades of difference. 'We didn't recognise the garden city as real Welwyn.' He had no such reservations about MK. He had worked in New Zealand and Australia for much of his life, and came back when his children grew up. He and his wife couldn't afford to live in exurban Hertfordshire now, but they could live in Milton Keynes.

I walked across to St Mary's church. Just inside the gate were three recent graves of young children, aged eleven months, two and six. Half hidden by trees was a high crucifix in memory of Elisabeth Edwardes, 'daughter of William third Baron Kensington', who died, a world and an era away, in 1911. A leaflet on the parish notice board offered copies of *Milton Keynes is Different: The Story of the Ecumenical Movement in Milton Keynes, 1967–2005*, by Canon Robin Baker, price £6.75. St Mary's is admired for its Perpendicular east window and its spectacular twelfth-century chancel. Such churches grew, unplanned, from the earliest Norman structure through restoration and new wall paintings of the 1880 and on to High Church additions of the twentieth century. They can handle, also, Canon Baker's all-purpose, flat-pack theology. That is how suburbs classically grow. The Church of England's parish churches are, in their way, the suburbia of religion: mild, pretty, friendly-up-to-a-point.

Milton Keynes always advertises itself as the newest of the new, though the strata of its history are beginning to accumulate. It is acquiring a CV, not just a birth certificate. It is still a PR man's paradise. The mirrored glass of the rail station. The artificial lakes with their windsurfers, bandstand and Peace Pagoda (ah, those were the days). The Gulliver's Land theme park. The Xscape indoor ski run, like an inflated metallic armadillo. But scattered throughout MK are those little villages – brick cottages with neat-towered stone churches – which were here long before. In the big hall of the shopping mall, alongside bamboo jacuzzis and Honda lawn mowers ('The power of dreams'), a stall was selling cast-metal painted house-plates: Ivy Cottage, Cranford House, The Old Bakehouse, Puddleduck Cottage, Casa Rosa, Springbank and, curiously, St Thérèse.

But Milton Keynes does like novelty. Eco-novelty especially. In Solar Court, all the houses have solar panels. Milton Keynes got into sustainability very early. In another neighbourhood I saw some odd-looking green and black structures. I couldn't work out what they were. Going across, I found they were the home of a very enterprising body called MacIntyre, which tries to give the mentally handicapped a place in the ordinary world. The design was by Edward Cullinan. A neo-romantic architect like Cullinan – Richard MacCormac is another – fits well into the house-style of MK neighbourhoods, away from the commercial jazz of the centre. (Oscar Peterson's delicate piano versus the Woody Herman big band.) I had a cup of coffee in the MacIntyre café. Shop assistants swept the floor with slow, extreme care. The cakes were baked on the premises. Upstairs they were weaving a stock of rugs to sell. In the greenhouses behind, I bought three geraniums. The buildings that had caught my eye were divided into special flats.

When MacIntyre was built, twenty years ago, there would have been an outcry, in any other city, from edgy property owners. It makes a difference that everything is so new. I talked to a young mother in a house across the road. She and her husband moved here because of London property prices; he commuted. 'I don't mind MacIntyre, why should I?' She, too, loved MK. The enthusiasm – itself very American, in a way – is catching. Friends of her had come now, because the city was so unpolluted, so Persil-clean.

The city centre began as an exercise in plain cuboid architecture, but anarchy then set in. The multiplex cinema, The Point, with bar, pin-tables and bingo, marked the new way. It was like a neon wigwam, as if someone had scribbled in red and yellow highlighter ink on a Ben Nicholson abstract. Now its mid-1980s exuberance is overshadowed by newer, bigger blocks. Unlike older city centres, MK's has no cheap property clustered around it. If you wait long enough, this will inevitably come. Meanwhile, even charitable ventures tend to be at the low-cost end of an industrial estate, in a black corrugated box, like an electronics firm.

Campbell Park was laid out at the opposite end of the shopping mall from the church, in a gesture to the formal Victorian idea of a city. I walked to the park's large round pond. The four outflows were labelled north, south, east, west. They are fond of that sort of thing in Milton Keynes, as if geography were a lifebelt to cling on to. Like some of the road names – Midsummer Boulevard, Silbury Boulevard, Saxon Gate – this touch of compass-point humour is an evocation of the folksy roots of early town planning. In honour of a newer, Americanised tradition, all main roads away from the centre are given a simple letter and number: V4, for example, runs roughly north–south, the V standing for 'vertical'; and H8 runs east–west, the H standing for 'horizontal'. (Historically, V4 is the old Roman road of Watling Street.) Unlike New York's Fifth Avenue and 42nd Street, the vertical-horizontal designations are an odd way to picture a city. It is as if Milton Keynes were a permanent wall chart. Perhaps a back-up to a management presentation.

In Campbell Park, the quality of the finish, as everywhere in Milton Keynes, is astonishing. This was the founding corporation's finest bequest. It never stinted on granite kerbstones, good paving, lavish planting of trees and bushes.

MK may have put its money on California-style mobility, and hoped with this to coax international businesses, but it has been built to last. Sculpture and statuary are scattered around with an almost Edwardian abandon. MK's most famous monument is the cluster of concrete cows in a field near the London–Birmingham railway line, where they gaze up at the passing Virgin trains. They were given to MK in 1978 by their sculptor Liz Leyh, the city's first 'artist in residence.' At the time, the city was only a rough sketch of what it was to become. It was mostly grassland. The borough's PR folk seem rather embarrassed by the cows now. Too jokey to put on a business plan? So far as I could see, they featured on none of MK's boosterish advertising. Nor did the locals seem very fond of them. They appeared to prefer the hyper-realistic bronzes of human figures in the city centre.

I thought I should check the cows out. They were hard to find, in a field across a stream, behind a housing estate. There were signposts to the very modest ruins of an abbey and a Roman villa, but nothing to point you to the cows. A young man in a bandana had offered to show me the way. He hopped into the car for a couple of hundred yards. 'I'm meeting some mates there,' he said, and waved in the right direction as he got out at a café.

I parked on Octavian Drive, at the junction with Hadrians Drive. This was a solid brick-built spec suburb of the 1970s and 1980s. All the residents I could see were shearing hedges or washing cars. I made a guess at which path to take, detoured round a stream, and made it. On the postcards I'd bought in WH Smith in the shopping mall the cows looked almost life-size. The camera always lies. In reality, they were quite small. Close up they were also very odd.

This photo-realist painting, entitled 'Fiction, Non-Fiction and Reference' (39 × 13 feet), by Boyd & Evans (1984), hangs in Milton Keynes' central library. It was painted as Milton Keynes got into its optimistic stride. An image of MK's ego? For a possible id, see overleaf.

These battered and repainted concrete cows were a popular image of Milton Keynes when sculpted by Liz Leyh in 1978, but have been shunned by twenty-first-century officialdom. Under-signposted and hard to find. Are these gloomy figures the city's id, as opposed to its ego (enshrined in Boyd & Evans's imagery on the previous page)?

They were twisted, even distorted, like images from a campaign protesting about bovine abortion, or cast-off old props from a horror movie. They were painted black and white, but you could see pinker paint through the scratches. They didn't look much loved. I saw that my guide had beaten me to it. He and his two friends were standing in the middle of the group of six cows. When he left, another teenager came along. All three sat on the cows, with their mobile phones. It seemed like an odd place to meet up. The cows used to be very visible from the railway line to Birmingham. They are now almost entirely screened off by trees and bushes. In the central library, they have local history shelves of eighteenth-century parish registers: the marriage of Edw. Savage to Eliz. Keen, and of Thos. Jacob to Martha Potter. But Liz Leyh's suburban cows are the first items in Milton Keynes's real history that will have to go in a museum.

Along the Grand Union Canal, with its alders and swans, you saw the MK idyll, as advertised. Dearer housing surrounded a marina with private jetties. A pub was full of imitation barge-ware and bright young women sipping orange juice. A notice requested 'smart casual' clothes. At one of the houses, I rang the doorbell and interrupted a manager, divorced and between jobs, and a neighbouring wife, having a morning cup of coffee together. He was in grey suit and spotted tie. She was in a pink tracksuit. He was keen to tell me of all the local ventures he was involved in: Neighbourhood Watch and the rest. She seemed less certain about Milton Keynes. 'I know a young woman along here who won't go out on her own. The thick planting gives people chance to hide and jump out.' She looked back with regret to her old home in a Home Counties village. Many houses in MK, she told me, were bought for investment, not for living in. 'Milton Keynes is the biggest sexual turn-off there is,' the man suddenly said.

I walked past a cement dinosaur to another terrace. A retired civil servant was polishing his car. He came here fifteen years ago, he said, because he couldn't afford to live in Hastings. This surprised me slightly. A rather run-down resort, with poor transport links, Hastings had a reputation, among Londoners at least, as a cheap place that was coming up in the world. He explained to me the lengthy walks he and his wife could make along the city's network of parks and canals. 'We saw a kingfisher here yesterday.' He came as a tenant; but, helped by discounts, he then bought the house. A sleepy woman in her early twenties came to another door in a floppy white dressing gown. She explained that she worked nights 'in catering'. She had lived in Milton Keynes since she was twelve. 'It's all right. Just like anywhere else, I expect.'

Even in Milton Keynes, where conscience and commerce have made every effort to create the good life, the id will out. The window panel in one door was broken. On the wall beside it, in purple paint, it said: 'Filthy Pigs'. On the door, it said: 'Please knock LOUD'. When I did, there was a great racket of dogs barking. Loren came out to talk to me, tearful and puffy. She looked to be in her early forties, with short greying hair and scratch marks on her face. Kids had done the paint, she said: 'the youngest eight, the oldest twelve'. They had also thrown egg at her window. Looking up, I could see the streaks. 'A man started climbing over my fence in the night. I screamed

A fine dust of social difference settles over Milton Keynes. Above: The top of the ladder – repro farmsteads at Shenley Church End (1980s), built by Bovis. Opposite: The bottom of the ladder – Beanhill, MK's earliest housing for rent, designed by Norman Foster Associates and others (1970s).

and screamed.' She had two dogs and three cats. One of the cats 'can sit so still, you'd look at the mantelpiece and think, "What a beautiful statue".' She moved here from Netherfield when a previous cat was shot dead with an airgun. She paid for her freezer, her television and a few other things to come over by van. 'Everything else went by shopping trolley.'

While we talked, a small white van pulled up. 'That's all I need.' It was the RSPCA. A neighbour had reported her. The uniformed van driver spoke to her pleasantly but firmly about a dog of hers that wouldn't put on weight. 'I do feed him. I do,' she said. 'It may be diabetes,' the man thought, or said he thought. 'You must try to get him to the vet.' Loren said she would, and the man filled in his job sheet and went off.

Loren was German. Her husband had left her. She was on her way now to a cleaning job. Otherwise, she hadn't worked for ten years. Thinking back to her dead cat and her vandalised wall, she said: 'They just don't have control over kids now. The fathers just watch.' I waved goodbye to Loren as she went down an underpass with her shopping bag to catch the bus. 'It's just because I talk funny,' she said.

Suddenly, suburban Milton Keynes began to seem like any other city. It has a jailhouse: Woodhill prison for the toughest, category-A criminals, opened in 1992. A financially challenged soccer club, the Wimbledon Dons, was bought up and now, as the MK Dons, they have a bright new stadium. Mark Clapson subtitled his social history of Milton Keynes 'Middle England/ Edge City'. Milton Keynes sums up what is new about cities. From being a fine 1960s experiment, it has settled down into being one of the bigger, more prosperous towns in this part of the Midlands.

The shopping mall – which Milton Keynes was built around – has all the usual suspects: John Lewis, Boots, Marks & Spencer. Tired shoppers sat, texting, under the potted palm trees. A nail bar offered temporary tooth jewels for only £10. The main hall advertised a couple of forthcoming tea dances. (At Campbell Park, the 'Proms in the Park' event offered Jools Holland and his Rhythm and Blues Orchestra.) There

was an outdoor market behind the mall, packed with stalls. An African mother and her daughter hovered next to the 'ex-catalogue clearance sale' of watches: 'all £2'. The smell of cheap hotdogs and chips wafted downwind from a pair of trailers. Cut-price bras were £3.99 each, two for £7, three for £10. Fishing rods were £22.50. Many of the stallholders were Pakistani. A young woman with her husband and small daughter walked happily through the hubbub. 'It's just like Birmingham, innit?' she said.

Some families have been here long enough to have networks of intermarriage with other families. One of these days, a Milton Keynes accent may emerge. So far, almost any sound emerged when locals opened their mouths. It remains a city of immigrants – though not in the inner city sense. It was 91 per cent white at the 2001 census. People of Indian origin were the largest non-white group (more than 3,000 of them); there was also a notably large group of Chinese (1,835). Both are groups well known, rightly, for keeping their heads down and getting on with things. Not surprisingly, Milton Keynes has an immigrant air of energy and enterprise. It is a city of trees, of houses and of jobs (colossal sheds with baffling names like Amscan or Dwell). It is the latest tribute to the vigour and variety of suburbia.

11. PLAN OR NO PLAN

For the ultimate place with a plan, take the train to Beaconsfield, and walk the few yards from the station to the model village of Bekonscot. Since it was founded in 1929, 14 million people, mostly children, have visited it. But beware: here are terrible (but very satisfactory) puns, well up to the standard of the *Beano* in its heyday, and outdoing *Viz* today. A baker called Ivan Huven. A florist called Dan D. Lyon. A greengrocer called Chris P. Lettis. A milkman called Phil D. Churn. A butcher's shop called Sam & Ella. The English are obsessed with word-jokes, and Bekonscot is nothing if not English.

The oddity of this village, in a 40,000 square foot Buckinghamshire field, had to be seen to be believed. I went round it like Gulliver among the Lilliputians – or like a planner deciding how lesser folk should live. The tallest church spire reached only to my knees. When an accountant called Roland Callingham began Bekonscot as a hobby, it was only slightly nostalgic. He had the same love for a vanishing Home Counties England as George Orwell and the Williams-Ellises. Even now, latter-day intrusions, like the salmonella joke, were rare. Non-jokily, the tiny football team now had four non-white players. But male spectators still wore flat caps. The village coalman was I.M. Black.

The Bekonscot theatre starred the music hall innuendo specialists, Max Miller and George Formby. The star singer was Gracie Fields. Top of the bill at the dwarf cinema was, inevitably, *Snow White*. Forges made horseshoes in the 1930s, as they still do in Bekonscot's miniature version. They hadn't yet become desirable residences called The Old Forge. The only chain store I could see in the Bekonscot dream was Marks & Spencer, which in its early high-street days was only a notch or two above Woolworth's. Not a superstore in sight. There was a coalmine, with a whirring wheel. A young mother with a northern accent pulled her daughter across to see, and told her: 'Granddad used to work here. That's where he went down.'

Enid Blyton lived in Beaconsfield, and was a patron of the model village. Her Famous Five, like Richmal Crompton's William, would have felt at home here. When Blyton's own house, Green Hedges, was sold off to developers after her death – and replaced by a cul-de-sac of half a dozen smaller houses called Blyton Close – Bekonscot built a replica in tribute. A little Blyton figure

Opposite: Temporary squat, Wandsworth Eco Village, south London (1990s). Built with recycled timber on the site of a former Guinness brewery.

The village green at Bekonscot, Buckinghamshire. Enid Blyton territory. This toy village, beloved by young children, includes a replica of her house, with a tiny figure of Noddy on the doorstep.

sits on a garden seat, with a portable typewriter on its sensibly skirted knee. Bekonscot specialises in a managed version of sensibleness. Tennis is played in hats and long white dresses. At the farm they gather corn into stooks. The riskiest item in the funfair is a helter-skelter. Gypsies sit in a dell and one of them plays a fiddle. Ronald Callingham walked through Bekonscot twice a day, on his way to and from the station. It was a commuter's dream of heaven. Outside Bekonscot, all, all are gone, the old familiar faces.

Where do dreams go when they die? One answer is: to Bekonscot. Here, in the tradition of children's comics down the years, everything was a non-threatening joke. The headmaster at the primary school was listed as I. Kane MA. A fleeing fox was safely stationed several feet ahead of the huntsmen and the hounds. The local solicitors, Messrs Argue & Twist, were not about to sue the school under the Human Rights Act, or pursue the hunt for cruelty to animals. There were no screaming police patrol cars, no helicopter. The only aircraft in the sky was a propeller-driven biplane, held up by an obvious wire, and perhaps beginning its journey to Croydon airport. Tinplate ads, as you walked along the paths, said it was a 'Lovely day for a Guinness'. They assured you that 'Players please' – and to prove it a saucy red-lipsticked Wren puffed away at a long white 'Navy Cut' cigarette.

Planning Bekonscot, which sits there neatly like a little biological specimen, is one thing. Planning the less malleable real world is something much tougher, and much more liable to unfortunate side-effects. The high point of urban and rural planning in Britain, the 1947 Town and Country Planning Act, nationalised land development rights. This had echoes of feudalism, when all land in the last resort belonged to the king, and everyone below him held it only on a system of sufferance and irrevocable duties (called feus). Under the 1947 Act, ownership of the land itself was left with individuals and firms, but what they might wish to do with it was prescribed from above. In the last analysis, if they resisted, there was the possibility of compulsory purchase. Land ownership after 1947 no longer meant quite what it had done twenty years before.

This is not to claim that ownership meant nothing. When the National Trust was founded in 1895, as one of Britain's most enduring and most admirable institutions, it based its protection of threatened landscapes on the purchase and ownership of land. The model was the way that Hampstead Heath had been saved from being built over in the late Victorian house-building boom. The heathland had been bought, by philanthropists and other subscribers, from the money-grubbing landowner. In the twenty-first century the National Trust reasserted its desire to go on buying land for this purpose, after a decades-long detour into buying aristocratic mansions. The trust had been coaxed into this rival, and very expensive, commitment by a peerage groupie called James Lees-Milne. It turns out to have been only an episode in the trust's beneficent history.

Even the trust has had to yield to government prescription sometimes. In the late twentieth century, the long-contested Okehampton bypass in Devon smashed through a protected wood; and some of the Channel Tunnel approach was built on National Trust land outside Folkestone. Both routes were more for the benefit of tourists than anyone else, thus underlining the priorities of a new economy. The Okehampton case is an ironic example of the risks of top-down planning. The route south of the town, and through Bluebell Wood, was forced through by government because an alternative route north of the town would have meant cutting into 'irreplaceable' farmland. By the time the new road was actually built, agriculture had become such a chancy business that the farm owners would have been delighted to sell some of their fields for road construction. By then the plan was immutably fixed. The road went through the middle of a wood that had been bequeathed to the trust 'in perpetuity'.

Of all the nationalisations, land development nationalisation is a rare example that has endured, more or less unchanged. Before the Brown government's emergency nationalisation of the Northern Rock bank in 2008, these state takeovers had mostly been enacted by the 1945–51 Labour administration – though a Central Electricity Generating Board and an all-powerful Milk Marketing Board dated back to 1926 and 1933 respectively, and were set up under Conservative-dominated ministries. The generating board's pylons grid gave birth to verses, mostly long forgotten, by leftist poets. In 1933, as the grid was all but complete, one of the best-known, Stephen Spender, eulogised the gaunt steel structures on which the neo-baroque architect Reginald Blomfield was the design consultant. Spender saw the pylons as 'Bare like nude, giant girls that have no secret' – which raised a few questions about how many naked women Spender had, at that point, ever seen. (Lenin had said: 'Communism is Soviet power plus the electrification of the whole country.' A technological target still not achieved by the time the USSR was wound up on 31 December 1991.) For its part, the Milk Marketing Board helped to prop up farmers' prices, but it also destroyed for decades their freedom to sell new varieties of cheese.

Planning was always about far, far more than land. In *Postwar*, his far-reaching history of Europe from 1945 to 1989, Tony Judt points out that planning was 'the political religion of postwar Europe'. The assumption, on all sides and in all countries, was that 'If democracy was to work, if it was to recover its appeal, it would have to be *planned*.' This advocacy didn't follow from the Soviet example – of disastrous and murderous five-year plans. Only the local Communist parties argued for such supposed panaceas. Only in Soviet-controlled eastern Europe did these parties have the opportunity, or more precisely the obligation, to carry them out within their own frontiers. The alternative idea was to have a democratic form of planning.

The vogue for planning had roots long before 1945. In Britain, Judt locates them in pre-1914 liberal reformism, when the nineteenth-century caretaker state was felt to be outmoded. At first, the cry was mainly for progressive taxation, protection of labour, and sometimes state ownership of some so-called natural monopolies. (Even so, it is often forgotten that gas, electricity and water supply in Britain had long been controlled by municipalities, and health care by municipalities and charities. Nationalisation tore the heart out of local government in Britain. It never recovered.) Events changed that first modest limit on the demand for more planning. The first was the introduction of conscription, in 1916, after the earlier disasters of the First World War had made it impossible to rely on a volunteer army. This was the greatest-ever intrusion by the state into the life of the ordinary British citizen. Once that Rubicon was crossed, the intrusiveness became a constant temptation. The interwar collapse of the international economy buttressed the case for intervention. In the Second World War, this became a habit. Faced with Hitler's Germany, Winston Churchill's Conservative-led wartime coalition gave itself permission to do absolutely anything it wanted. Under the Emergency Powers (Defence) Act, 1940, it could direct anyone to do anything, could control any property, and could assign any industrial plant to fulfil any purpose it decided on. This was a cast of mind that it took a very long time even partly to shake off.

'What planning was really about,' Judt writes, 'was faith in the state.' In Britain, he maintains, 'very little actual *planning* ever took place, the real issue was *control* – of industries and social and economic services – through state ownership as an end in itself.' Certainly the unique attempt at a National Plan, in 1965 – under a government led by Attlee's former trade minister Harold Wilson – was a noted political debacle. It was abandoned as soon as begun. But where there *was* planning, in every sense, was in the development or non-development of land.

Clough Williams-Ellis was far from alone in his onslaughts on interwar semis and bungalows. Paul Oliver, Ian Ross and Ian Bentley chronicled these innumerable attacks and their consequences, in regretful but entertaining detail, in *Dunroamin: The Suburban Semi and its Enemies*. As so often, those who attack something with most violence do so partly because, despite themselves, they feel, or have felt, the tug of its appeal. One of the most charming books on the delights of suburbia is J.M. Richards's *The Castles on the Ground*. This was published in 1946, with illustrations by John Piper. Richards had begun it, out of nostalgia for England, when he was away in Egypt, Palestine and Lebanon on war work. He wrote in his foreword: 'If the scenes described have been unnaturally intensified by being seen, as it were, through the wrong end of a telescope, I hope that at least something of what is significant has been brought out along with what is most clearly remembered.'

To him, writing from far away, the suburb *was* England. It was 'a living thing, continually revitalised as it responds to urges in the immediate present.' He was unworried by the mishmash of designs: 'Architectural symbols have to be reinterpreted as social symbols. An elaborate code has grown up, instinctively understood by those whom it concerns, by means of which family circumstances are depicted and achievements recorded in architectural language, almost after the fashion of heraldry.' The first instinct of the suburban dweller, he argued, 'is his craving for economic security, and, in a world that does nor provide this, for a defence that is always close at hand against the knowledge that he is at the mercy of elements which he cannot in the least control. That he is able to

Placing a New Town at Basildon was intended to get rid of the many self-help plotlands homes. The remaining few now feature on a heritage trail. The Haven, plotlands bungalow, Dunton Heath, Basildon.

take refuge from the implications of such knowledge in the domestic charms of a manufactured environment is a tribute to his typically English capacity for hand-to-mouth happiness and to his optimism, a virtue which far outweighs the concomitant vice of self-deception.'

Richards returned to Britain to pursue his profession as architecture critic (long-time editor of the *Architectural Review* and architectural correspondent of *The Times*) and all-purpose panjandrum (on the board of the 1951 Festival of Britain, adviser to the British Council, member of a governmental committee to reform traffic signs). At this point he reverted to Modernist dogma about both design and planning. Such is the potency of peer-group pressure.

You could argue that the nationalisation of all development rights was a sledgehammer to crack a nut. The policy's continuation, and the passions which have grown up around it, are astonishing, given its very limited successes. Its unhelpful side-effects are widespread. After all, for centuries the country had somehow rubbed along without land planning. Speculative builders had created

almost all the most admired townscapes, whether Georgian, Regency, Victorian or Edwardian. (To these I would add interwar suburbia.) They got many things wrong, inevitably – mostly, a recurrent obsession with building for the middle classes. But even this had its benefits. Until the gentrifications of the 1950s to 1970s, most of the huge town houses of Notting Hill, for example, had never been used as intended – as single-family homes. For lack of such buyers, they were let off by the floor or the room. Growing up there, John Bird, later the founder of the *Big Issue* newspaper, remembered it as an Irish slum. Cheap, rule-less property has its uses in a city.

The widespread building of highly regulated publicly funded and bureaucratically controlled council (or 'social') housing turned out to bring major problems of its own. The merits of smallness of scale, and flexibility and variety of use, were all too often forgotten. In a 2008 issue of the National Trust magazine – at which point its director was Fiona Reynolds, a former head of the Campaign to Protect Rural England – two photographs were juxtaposed.

A 'bender' dwelling: tarpaulin stretched over hazel poles and lined with blanket, with a wood-burner stove. King's Hill Collective, near Glastonbury, Somerset (1990s). It won planning permission as a low-environmental-impact site.

A home is for improving. Opposite page, above left: Stone cladding, new windows, Hendon, north west London. Middle left: Garden wall art, Chelmsford, Essex. Below left: Major works, Winchmore Hill, north London. Above right: Loft conversion, new porch, Mayfield Road, Bath. Below right: A 1930s semi is transformed, Dollis Hill. This page, above: Loft conversion lorry, 'Don't move out – Move up!!', Bristol. Middle: Bathland van, 'Inspiration to Installation', Mayfield Avenue, Kenton. Below: Decorator's van, Bromley.

An old boat hauled onto dry land beside the River Deben, converted into living quarters. Felixstowe Ferry, Suffolk.

'almost every village may have existed by the later eleventh century', but his proviso is important: 'not necessarily with the shape it has now'. What didn't work was abandoned. On the hilltop above Millais's celebrated painting of a blind girl, a rainbow vanishes behind the roofs of the Sussex village of Winchelsea. This is a potent example of an early planned town that failed. It is comparable to the *bastide* towns that the English kings set down all over south-west France. Half its street grid is empty, and the church was never finished.

Landscape and architecture – or, more precisely, landscape and building – have grown together in symbiosis. Even the spreading tentacles of suburban semis respected the spirit of the place they were built in. Under Voysey's distant and commercialised influence, they hugged the lie of the land. As for the mansions of the lords and squires, they were usually, in Hoskins's words, 'a warmth of red brick, a flash of stucco, among luxuriant trees' (a pre-echo of Milton Keynes?). The baroque in England was a foreign flower and not much appreciated, as Abel Evans's epitaph for Vanbrugh, architect (with Hawksmoor) of Blenheim Palace, showed:

Lie heavy on him, Earth! For he
Laid many a heavy load on thee!

The English see their landscape as like an apple. They have not, in the past, seen it as something never to be touched; but they did not want it bruised. Baroque is brutal. The first heroic stretch of the M1 was built in 1958–9 almost like a railway, in as straight a line as it could be, even through the Dunstable Downs. The harsh concrete bridges of the architect and engineer Owen Williams did nothing to relieve its fierceness. But later British motorways have seldom cut a swathe through the countryside in the way that the *autoroutes* (and the high-speed rail lines) do in France. So many of Williams's first bridges have now been demolished that the remainder almost count as ancient monuments.

Consider what positive planning has done to our towns and cities, and ask: 'Without planning could it conceivably have been worse?' Acre after acre of perfectly re-usable houses was demolished, under schemes for comprehensive development, to be replaced by high-rise blocks, failed 'streets in the sky', and unappealing estates of public housing which failed to generate the much-touted sense of community, partly because they ignored existing street-lines. About this the New Urbanists are quite right. Streets are a city's memory. Erase them, and it is hard, and often impossible, to recapture the same urban spirit. It is a form of architectural lobotomy.

This was one failed planning doctrine. Another is still with us. It is that, in spite of the obvious preference of most people – given the chance – for a suburban way of life, housing should be packed in within the old city boundaries, on sites which were never seen as good locations for homes. Where possible, it was ordained, these homes should be built as flats, over-riding the popular preference for free-standing houses. Those flats that were 'social housing,' then became transit zones, often for new arrivals to Britain. Those built for private ownership were often bought as buy-to-let by amateur investors who, during the late twentieth century and early twenty-first century housing price boom, thought that this was a sure-fire way to make money. (They learnt the hard way.) In general, the restrictions imposed by planning rules and by governments fearful of Nimbyism meant that, in an era of rising national wealth, we built fewer houses than at any time since the 1920s. Constraint was the watchword. The freedoms of suburbia were trammeled.

As people grew wealthier, they started to wish for more space. (The same aspirations then kicked in, further down the income scale.) Many future projections for how many homes we may eventually need, and what kind of home, exaggerate the effect of 'singleton' households: the divorced, the separated, the gays not in a civil partnership. Such households do not always wish to have tiny amounts of space. Many of them would like to have space in which family or friends could stay for a few days. Others have demands for workspace, either permanently or for part of the time. In the meantime, household equipment has grown bigger and more complex: after the fridge and washing machine, the dishwasher, the dryer, the plasma TV, the laptop, the printer. The more drivers are charged for on-street parking, the more firmly they will ask for an off-street parking space. Even those who will be satisfied with a tight-knit flat in a close-packed estate from Monday to Friday increasingly seek a respite: somewhere out of the city where they can go from Friday evening until Monday and bolted together, could cost you up to £200,000 on a really good site. 'But it's freedom, isn't it?' one man told me. 'You step out of the door into your own little bit of dirt.' *Floreat suburbia*. Mobile homes are one answer for some of the new homes we shall need.

Every site had its own character, I found. At Swanbridge Park, I talked to one owner whose brasses were polished, her ceramic flower-girls neatly set out. But the park itself, though friendly, was slightly scruffy, tucked in behind a trading estate. Every home here had its net curtains. Some had stove-pipe chimneys. Others had pitched roofs added. One site was empty: a concrete slab, with two plastic pipes (narrow for water, wide for sewage), waiting for the next lorry delivery.

At another park, nearer the bottom of the scale, notices warned you: 'Live Cables Overhead' and 'Keep Dogs on Leash'. A car was jacked up on its front wheels. Young families jostled against older couples. A woman of almost eighty, a former chief petty officer, said: 'Myself, my husband, my father and my mother, we notched up seventy-six years in uniform between us. But for what?' This was like the Doncaster territory that Fran Abrams explored. If more cheap suburbs had been built, this trailer site would probably not be here.

Back in Oaklands' trailer-park suburbia, I rang the doorbell of a Lissett 'Oakwood' model, '38 by 20, two bedrooms, lounge, dining area, bathroom, kitchen, shed, many extras', on sale for £65,000. The owner was sitting on the sofa of the red and cream three-piece suite, watching the cricket. His wife was out walking the little dog whose photograph was on the glass-fronted cabinet. He was a retired engineer from north Wales: pale hair, blue acrylic shirt, very neat. I admitted I wasn't here to buy, but he amicably explained all the benefits. Almost everything was either made out of uPVC (windows and door frames, cornices) or coated in it (interior doors). 'So nothing could be easier. Maintenance is simplicity itself.' The double-glazing, he assured me, was the best that money could buy. The master bedroom had heated wardrobes and an en-suite shower. They moved south to be near friends, but the couple had died, soon after each other. 'Sad, but it's one of those things.' His wife now wanted to go back to north Wales. It would be another mobile home if they could find a park they liked. 'It took us three and a half years to find this one,' he said. 'It's the best in the area.' He wanted something of the same again. Suburbia, of which mobile home parks are one variation, is about choosing for yourself; and about choosing the self you want to be.

The mobile home: omnipresent but often unnoticed. Examples from west Sussex: Selsey (above) and Houghton, beside the River Arun (below).

12. PAST, PRESENT, FUTURE

The enemies of suburbia are forever at the gate. So far, at least. But it is time to drive them away. The recent omens have not been good. In the London Plan of 2002 – subtitled: *Spatial Development Strategy for Greater London* – there was a brief line stating that the plan 'should not attempt to dictate lifestyles'. But the verbal softener was not borne out by the rest of the text. This was markedly anti-suburban. There was strong encouragement for 'intensification' – in other words, trying to rebuild suburban houses and centres at higher densities. The pronunciamento was: 'London must become more compact.' This partly stemmed from the then mayor's determination to absorb the capital's rising population within the existing city boundaries. Outside central London, 'densities between 30 and 150 dwellings per hectare [between about 12 and 60 to an acre] can be achieved,' it was stated, by building flats and close-packed terrace-housing. The preference was for the upper end of this scale. There was an admirable ambition that the designs should make no discernible distinction between the appearance of different housing types – that is, between public and private. But this seemed – like much of the plan – to come under the heading of wishful thinking.

Great weight was put on the opportunities offered by Thames Gateway: all that polluted, former industrial land. Before he was ousted by Boris Johnson, Mayor Livingstone said that his support for the 2012 Olympics bid for a Stratford East site was driven by a desire to draw more government investment into this enormous terrain. It soon emerged that the hopes for Thames Gateway would be hard to fulfil. It wasn't long before a Housing Corporation special commission was warning of the low quality and poor location of much that was being built or planned. The commission reminded the Thames Gateway's planning officials that much of the area was already 'littered with examples of large, isolated and difficult estates with poor links to jobs, poor environments, poor services and poor transport'. Already, the commission said, there was 'a surfeit of hyper-dense flats, enabled by naïve and sometimes over-generalised planning'. Returning from Dagenham, I saw a fine example in two dominant high blocks of buy-to-let starter homes, erected next to the Gants Hill Tube

Waterlooville: a suburban satellite of Portsmouth, the epitome of pleasant, unassuming place to live and a running theme in the illustrations to this chapter. Denounced by interwar anti-suburbia campaigners, it continued to grow. Opposite: This example of garage-art patriotism echoes the town name's commemoration of a never forgotten national victory.

station in east London. They were completely out of scale with the surrounding avenues of modest semis. I was looking at the slums of the near future.

The commission recommended more planning. But the long-lived, plan-less model of suburbia was a much better bet. This building tradition has always been directly focussed on what people want, rather than on what (according to someone else) they 'ought' to want. The desire to cram people into flats has an inglorious history. The first Victorian opponents of London's East End slums built blocks of flats. These were all walk-up, with a single shared cold water tap on the open landings. The builders were such well-meaning organisations as the '4 per cent Industrial Dwellings Company'. (The idea was for charity to make a decent return on capital.) The blocks have nearly all been pulled down. The end-result of shifting people into flats has been to make them determined to get out as soon as they could afford it. In its own way, it encouraged the flight towards enjoying the freedoms of suburbia. This isn't what was, or is, intended.

Could a preference for Non-Plan be any worse than the failures of almighty Plan? It hardly seems so. Non-Plan is non-doctrinaire. Plan is in thrall to some overt or covert set of presumptions about how other people should live. Non-Plan favours flexibility and adaptability. Plan prefers rigour. A plan is often thought of as 'fulfilled', when it has merely been completed. There is seldom any thorough check on whether its aims have really been achieved. Almost all architectural designs suffer from the same drawback. The wish is mistaken for the deed.

The origins of plans are sometimes very odd. Successive London plans, for example, pursued the idea that the capital should be re-shaped into strictly self-contained neighbourhoods, divided from one another by traffic-only road systems. This was not how traditional London grew. That is why many main roads and streets are still lined by shops, houses, public libraries, churches and town halls. The new idea had its origin in two books on town planning published in 1938 and 1943 by a retired Scotland Yard policeman with the strange name of Alker Tripp. His main interest was in road traffic control. Perhaps he also hoped that his scheme would cut down crime. In fact, like 'streets in the sky', it would make villains' getaway easier. Fortunately, much of London proved resistant to this change. But anyone driving out east along the A12 or A13 towards Essex can see that the general rule – you try out your planning ideas on the working classes – has continued to be true. New Towns became, and remain, the most ardent Trippists.

I am no Dr Pangloss. I don't claim that suburbia is an example of the Leibnitizian creed which Voltaire so ferociously parodied: that 'all is for the best in the best of all possible worlds'. Obviously some suburbs have become run-down. Others will become run-down in the future. That is the way cities are. The suburbs may not be the best that humanity can devise. But the pursuit of the supposed best has a habit of becoming dictatorial. The best is, notoriously, the enemy of the good. For most people, most of the time, suburbia is as good as it gets.

A bungalow as the base for a small Waterlooville business. Bayview Doves specialises in 'white dove release' for 'weddings, anniversaries, funerals, memorials, birthdays, grand openings'.

This is not to say that suburbs fall into the same pattern worldwide. In many cities in western Europe, for example, certain suburbs have become places to put your immigrants out of sight. Remember: this outcome was due to Plan, not Non-Plan. In outer Paris, this has produced various dens of crime. One of the first such estates to be built was Sarcelles, on the far north-eastern outskirts of Paris, beyond the *périphérique*. When I walked round it, I found it hard to persuade anyone to open their door. John Berger chronicled the fear and squalor in such suburbias in his 1999 Goya-inspired novel, *King: A Street Story*. The growing public anxieties helped Nicolas Sarkozy to become French president in 2007. Paris is not unique. In Amsterdam, I caught the train out towards the Bijlmer estate of public housing where, in 1992, an El Al transport plane had crashed into one of the blocks. Many of those killed were immigrants. I made the journey because I was puzzled by how few non-white faces I saw in central Amsterdam. I knew that the proportion in the general population was, statistically, much higher. Holland is often cited admiringly by visiting overseas architects (who, like other tourists, seldom stray far from urban centres). My Amsterdam journey was a revealing test-case.

As the train stopped at the stations along the line, and people got on or off, my fellow-passengers became less and less white. At the station for the estate, I seemed to be the only non-black person still on the train. Like so much architect-designed

Quiet days in Hampshire. Until the Second World War, Waterlooville was little more than a village; by 1930 the population was about 2,000; from the late 1950s to the early 1970s, it expanded rapidly. Above and opposite: 1960–70s houses. The population is now about 30,000.

public housing, the estate had looked very pretty in aerial photographs. I could see how it might appeal to local politicians and planners in a balsa-wood model laid out on a table, protected from dust by a Perspex cover. The design was a series of interlocked hexagons, like part of a honeycomb. At a glance, all very aesthetic. At ground level, it was an oppressive nightmare. The inhabitants had barricaded themselves in. One flat was still devoted to a shrine to those killed in the crash. All the other flats seemed to be lived in. I spoke to a community warden and asked him why this was so. In most British cities, I said, these would have become 'hard to let' flats, with many vacancies. Here, a plan seemed to take care of any grievance the residents had with the flats. 'There is no other option,' the warden said.

Most forms of suburbia create no special aesthetic pattern, seen from the air. They have the randomness you find in nature, rather than in art. Their main attraction, from that high angle, is their greenery: all those garden and trees. Apart from the suburbs designed by the state or by local authorities (whether British, French or Dutch), most were built piecemeal. The estates were, and are, intended to appeal individually, at ground level, to individuals. Why should this attract such anathemas, even now?

In *Dunroamin*, Paul Oliver and his co-authors ended their loving defence of semis with a telling quotation from a major exhibition of 1930s art and design, held at the Hayward Gallery, London, in 1980, and sponsored jointly by the Arts Council and the Victoria & Albert Museum. The photographs of architect-designed public housing looked notably grim to a non-architect eye: multi-storey flats in south London and inner Liverpool; regimented estates of Letchworth-type houses in London (the St Helier estate, the LCC's southside version of eastside Becontree/Dagenham) and in Manchester (Raymond Unwin's Wythenshawe). The exhibition had a less prominent sub-section on 'speculative housing'. Here were photographs of Rectory Gardens, Edgware, and of 'superior semi-detached homes, Becontree estate.' The more everyday version of the semi, the authors of Dunroamin noted, 'was represented by a single photograph entitled "The Promise of Suburban Bliss". Its caption read: "Victims of the Thirties building boom. The Borders family outside their jerry-built house, aptly named Insanity." Fifty years after, the Establishment of architects and critics clings tenaciously to its clichés.'

With this, the writers rested their case. Published in 1981, their book was thought worth reprinting in 1994. The clichés, unfortunately, are still all around us. 'Jerry-built' seems to mean 'built without the benefit of an architect'. Unlike many all-too-solid public estates, such as Hulme in Manchester, Nightingale in Hackney, Hyde Park in Sheffield (all 1960s) or Quarry Hill in Leeds (1930s) – which were all much admired by the architecture press in their day – hardly any semis have ever been demolished for any reason other than road schemes. The same durability, in the teeth of contempt by the experts, will be true of today's more cramped suburbia.

This is not just an argument about aesthetics. It is about the way people wish to live. Why should their wishes be trampled on, in the name of Plan? The misplaced abhorrence of suburbia caused some to welcome the switchback in oil prices in the early twenty-first century, in the hope that this would put an end to car-based housing estates. The odds are against this. The suburban impetus seems to be well-nigh universal. In 1985, in *Crabgrass Frontier*, Kenneth Jackson looked back at the oil price hikes of the 1970s. These led to great political and economic turmoil for a time. Governments fell. Firms went bankrupt. The growth of suburbia paused, but it did not stop. Jackson thought that, in the United States, the passion for suburbia was driven by both fear and love: fear of the city and love of the countryside. In a suburbia 'briefing' in 2008, the *Economist* spoke of the 'useful dullness of suburbs'. None of these psychological attractions have changed. In his 1995 book *Métapolis*, François Ascher wrote of cities as 'a mixture of indifference and tolerance. No one is a stranger; all are strangers.' This has its attraction for some people some of the time, and for a few people all of the time. It ought to be hard to argue that the suburban experience is intrinsically worse. This doesn't prevent to argument being put. In a trailer for a Radio 4 programme about suburbia, in August 2008, the *Daily Telegraph*'s radio critic noted that, by contrast with the town and the country, the suburb was, in every sense, 'the bit in the middle, the one everyone sneers at, apologises for, disowns'.

Slough is just down the M4 from Cranford, Middlesex. Being on the far side of the London green belt, Slough counts as an exurb, whereas Cranford is a suburb. The growth of both has been driven by their nearness to Heathrow. Slough is no one's conception of a pretty Thames Valley town. (If Elstree Studios wanted a background of Olde England, they always went to the Hertfordshire village of Letchmore Heath, not far from O'Connorville: population 470, pub on the green, no public transport at all. In the 1960 film adaptation of John Wyndham's alien-invasion novel, *The Midwich Cuckoos*, Letchmore Heath

'God is in the detail', Mies van der Rohe stated. In suburbia the details imply: 'Despite appearances, all these houses are different. And this is my very own house.' Above left: Pebbledash, Craigleith, Edinburgh. Above right: Diamond-paned leaded lights, Bromley. Middle left: 'Waney' (rough-cut) boarding and fake shutters, Bromley. Middle right: Sunburst gate, Chelmsford. Below left: Stained-glass landscape, front door, Cardiff. Below right: Quality Street lady, staircase window, Muswell Hill, north London.

Seen at the right angle, on the right day, you might think that this Waterlooville road was the countryside. Suburbia is the great compromise between privacy and price, and between town and country.

stands in as Midwich.) But Slough has been built around the prospect of work, not prettiness. After the First World War, a sharp-eyed entrepreneur bought an old army storage depot and turned it into the Slough Trading Estate. One of the first industrial arrivals was the British branch of Mars. I smelled chocolate in the air when I walked onto the estate. Betjeman, an ardent supporter of Modernism at the time, was disgusted by the place and wrote the 1930s poem which is quoted in every journalistic article about Slough:

> Come, friendly bombs, and fall on Slough
> It isn't fit for humans now ...

By the time the bombs became reality, he changed his mind about sprawl, whether in Slough or further afield. In June 1940, he told his BBC listeners: 'Before the war, I used sometimes to give talks on architecture and town planning, I remember referring to Swindon as a great octopus or starfish or something stretching out its tentacles of jerry-built houses into the quiet country (Swindon forgives me). But now I am so forgiving I *like* suburbs: nothing is ugly.' Slough has forgiven him, too. One 1990s office block in Slough bears the name Betjeman House.

In his broadcast, Betjeman said that, as he cycled round city suburbs, he had begun to see 'a strange beauty in those quiet deserted evenings with the few remaining children showing off in the evening sunlight.... Now the hedges are growing up and the trees are giving a greenness to it all. I see a beauty in it. I mean, they are there, those houses: they are part of England.' Contemplating suburbia, everyone has their favourite time of day. In *The Child in the City*, Colin Ward wrote: 'Regarded as a childhood idyll, the suburb is best in mid-afternoon. It is quiet and still and the only sounds are the sounds of childhood: an occasional shout from the playing-fields of the secondary school, singing heard through the windows of the primary school, and the cries of small children in the public gardens as their mothers chat over their baby-carriages. It is the child-rearing sector of the city: its nursery.' Ward even praised the unfinished nature of many suburbs. The fact that they were places in transition was an attraction, not a defect. 'The place that is *becoming*, the unfinished habitat, is rich in experiences and adventures for the child, just because of the plenitude of unmade bits of no-man's-land which have ceased to be agricultural and are not yet residential.' This

Waterlooville royalty.

appealing incompleteness became even more true with the economic recession which hit Britain in 2008. Construction firms laid off hundreds of workers and shut down on any new building work which wasn't within sight of being finished. Brick-making factories were mothballed.

Ward thought that a child would love the 'secret places for solitude', and would be 'reminded of the poignancy of time and change. Almost before his eyes the habitat alters.' François Ascher echoed this plea not to panic in the face of urban change: 'We mustn't think that, because towns are being transformed, they are thereby being destroyed.' Suburbia may have grown, but so has conservation. 'In Europe, at least,' he notes, 'we are preserving the physical appearance of old towns more than in earlier periods.' Of course, behind those preserved facades, nothing may be anything like the way it used to be, socially. You can't freeze-frame city life.

British governments from the late 1990s on were fatally infected by the propaganda of the anti-suburbanites: that elite combination of Nimbys, New Urbanists and ecologists. The long-time minister for housing John Prescott was especially vulnerable to such un-thought-through dreams of Olde England. He and his political colleagues took so long deciding that it would be a good idea to plan to build more houses that, by the time they did, the economic crash meant that they couldn't achieve even half the target they had set themselves. Historically, Non-Plan had been more responsive than Plan. In the early years of the twenty-first century, fewer houses were being built in Britain than at any time since the 1920s. Kate Barker's official report on the supply of housing, in 2004, rubbed in the obvious point that if you sit on the supply of land, and build few houses where they are needed, you increase the cost of the houses which are already there: almost all of them in the existing suburbs. The not-very-mysterious laws of supply and demand had been kidnapped, for a time, by the anti-suburbanites. Arguments about 'sustainability' became hardly concealed arguments against building anything. 'The aspiration for home ownership is as strong as ever,' Kate Barker (no relation of mine) wrote. Current policy was bringing about 'an ever widening economic and social divide'.

The haves were once more buttressed against the have-nots. 'Homes are more than shelter,' she pointed out. They are the 'entry ticket' to the kinds of services people wish to have, among the kinds of people they wish to live among. She recognised the dilemmas: each house built meant a certain total of square feet was no longer open land. Admittedly, not always for ever. This is demonstrated by the deserted minelands villages of County Durham in our own day, as it was by the changes in the eighteenth-century countryside evoked by Oliver Goldsmith's best known poem, 'The Deserted Village'. In both kinds of settlement, houses finally gave way to grass. Economic change moves on. Nothing is ever 100 per cent permanent, even if the process can take decades or even centuries.

Planning slows change down, often to a speed so low that it can hardly be measured. Or if it is swift, it is usually destructive: consider the postwar history of Liverpool, Bradford or Hull city centres. To walk with an open eye around most British cities and suburbs is to become convinced that it is better to yield, wherever possible, towards creating the kinds of home, in the kinds of places, that people themselves appear to prefer.

In Britain and elsewhere much has been made of a slight increase in the population totals in city centres, after generations of decline. But the move outwards into suburbs and exurbs has far outpaced this converse shift, even under the planners' would-constraints. In the special, and much-touted case of Manchester, hardly a single resident had lived in the city centre for at least two centuries. The story is all in Engels's *The Condition of the English Working Class* in 1845. As Cottonopolis, Manchester was a worldwide wonder. The great German neo-classical architect Karl Friedrich Schinkel made a special trip in order to sketch the chimneys of the cotton mills. They were, he judged, the contemporary equivalent of the Egyptian obelisks. Manchester handed the city centre over to the wealth producers: factories, warehouses and some shops. All these were eventually topped out by Alfred Waterhouse's extraordinary neo-gothic town hall.

By the middle of the twentieth century, the cotton trade in Britain was in collapse, outsold by countries such as India (whose own cotton trade Lancashire's factories had, earlier, destroyed). Manchester faced urban turmoil. But by good luck, rather than good planning, Manchester – unlike its wool trade equivalent, Bradford – never demolished its city centre. It was a close-run thing. The Mancunians made disastrous planning errors all around the centre. They created an urban desert and called it Plan. The city architect did draw up a scheme to demolish the centre, also, in favour of Corbusian blocks and boulevards. Luckily for its future, Manchester was slow off the mark. As urban fashions changed, its city centre was available for reuse. The change was led by, first, Chinese businessmen moving in from Hong Kong or London. They saw the value of those vacant warehouses and factories. The next colonists were gay men, who sought a new urban life in and around Canal Street, as celebrated in the Manchester-based TV series *Queer as Folk*. In Britain, this was the first urban impact of the 'pink pound'. In New York, in some of the downtown Greenwich Village streets Jane Jacobs celebrated, the pink dollar had already taken over (which was not quite what she had intended). The international Gay Liberation campaign, Stonewall, is named after a gay bar in Christopher Street that the New York police raided in June 1969. The customers and their friends discovered a new unity and fought back.

None of this urban change was planning-led, and it was all the better for it. Neglect has its uses. In London, two of the main tourist destinations, Covent Garden and Camden Lock, were created from the bottom up, unplanned. Grandiose planning schemes had collapsed. Properties were, for a time, almost worthless. Squatters moved in, where planners now feared to tread. The plans had envisaged (at Covent Garden) the most damaging sort of inner-city demolition and (at Camden Lock) a destructive inner-ring motorway. A few traces of both projects remain on the London street map, like memorials to a bygone era of (we must hope) great planning disasters. Hardly anything ever completely vanishes.

Whether the original incoming pioneers at Covent Garden and Camden Lock would have approved of these places ending up as beacons of the great urban shopping mania is a different matter. Was this what all the rebelliousness would lead to? But no revolution pans out as expected. In a way, that is the point of Non-Plan. It is permissive, not prescriptive. It is libertarian. It assumes you should forbid as little as you can, and permit as much as you can. It offers freedom.

Suburbia, and its younger exurban relative, offer the widest freedoms. In all humility, Michael Hebbert, though a professor of planning, gave his perceptive book on London the subtitle *More by Fortune than Design*. He wrote those words, in 1998, in open-minded admiration, not complaint. The suburbs of London are a humane creation to be proud of, not something to whinge about. The same is true of many other cities, both in Britain and, increasingly, worldwide.

To save misunderstanding, and to repeat myself, my pro-suburbanism and my advocacy of Non-Plan, do not mean that I am arguing that any and all open space should be built on. But I am arguing that we should be very modest and precise in our prohibitions. Small urban green spaces are often as valuable to people as large ones. A recent LSE study suggested that they are even more valuable. Yet, in the late twentieth and early twenty-first centuries, they were regularly built on. Sacrificed for some imposed ideal of city form: close-knit, apartment-based.

The arguments about density are often very simplistic. They are a camouflage screen that conceals a wish that no one else should build anything anywhere. The case for saving on carbon emissions by building more densely is very thin. It is true that, if new homes are very near to people's jobs, residents make shorter work (but not leisure) journeys. And they more often take public transport, rather than driving. But the likely effects are tiny, not least because the change will only apply to people living in brand-new homes. Projections like that in the London Plan for densities of up to 60 dwellings to an acre (150 per hectare) were stupendously misguided. In his polemic *The Land Fetish*, Peter Hall cited a detailed study by the consultants Llewelyn Davies that proved that you can't just keep ratcheting up the density of homes, and expect to make the same saving in land all along the rising graph of propinquity. To pack in more homes (if they are to be a tolerable place to live) also means allotting more space for schools, recreation, GPs' surgeries and local shops. Most of the gain comes from getting the density up to between 12 and 16 homes per acre (30 to 40 per hectare). This is remarkably similar to the density at which many existing suburbs are built. At higher densities the gains rapidly diminish. One important difference from the past is that, with the change in household sizes, far fewer people will now be living in each of these new homes.

Wishful thinking prevails. If 100,000 people a year continued to leave London for outer suburbia or exurbia, they were voting with their feet against the plan's wish to corral all new homes within the political boundaries of the Greater London Authority. Many of the new homes that have been built within the GLA area have been occupied by newcomers to London from overseas. Their demands, for the time being, may be limited. You can bet that, with growing prosperity, they will follow the old pattern of ambition. And such ambitions point towards suburbia. Humane planning cannot rely on brainwashing.

None of this is peculiar to Britain. Suburbs are as changeable as city centres. The much-mocked Levittowns show how even the sharpest-priced, least 'aesthetic', suburbs will evolve. The *Economist* reported on the New Jersey Levittown at its

Waterlooville street-signs, here and on the next page, offer a pot-pourri of childhood memories: The Wind in the Willows, Winnie the Pooh, and Rupert Bear.

Toad and Ratty might feel aggrieved that their names were left out. Not quite the right ring?

fiftieth anniversary. The name had been changed to Willingboro years ago. Its residents were all white, when it was built. By 2008 two thirds were black. The Levittowns were emblematic of an enduring change towards out-of-town living. The change was, at the time, much feared. In 1960, fewer Americans lived in suburbs than in central cities or the countryside. By the end of the twentieth century, the reverse was true. Between 1990 and 2006, the *Economist* noted, the city of Chicago added 50,000 residents, reversing a long decline. But in those same years, 'the sprawling metropolis outside the city proper grew by well over a million'.

This fits well into François Ascher's analysis of the French metapolis. Everywhere in Europe, most outside visitors make their way inwards from the airport or the central rail station towards the 'old' city. Tourists, at least. Business visitors are likely to be met by a chauffeured car for a non-radial journey to some out-of-town company HQ. The old city is spruced up for the tourists, and for the old city's increasingly middle class inhabitants. Inner Paris may look much the same way as it did in, say, 1950. The population has drastically changed. The vast majority of people who would still call themselves 'Parisians' don't live here. They are in the suburbs and exurbs.

Suburbia, along with its exurban cousin, has become the greatest zone of growth – in living, in working and in creative vigour. This comes about in the teeth of all attempts to divert such growth. We should welcome this as a thriving example of individual choice. Non-Plan is struggling through, against the odds. The supposed social ill-effects have been constantly exaggerated. The suburbs, even the exurbs, are a vital component of the city. The semis of Kenton or Bromley, the malls at Lakeside and Bluewater: these are as important to present-day London as Trafalgar Square or Pall Mall. They are far more important – whatever the architecture journals say – than the Modernists' Barbican or Roehampton high-rise flats. We have been trapped before in the argument for greater density. The quest always ends up being abandoned, leaving ruins behind. The difficulties of forcing people to live all too close to other people, when they would rather not, become all too apparent. Both Mayfield Avenue in Kenton, and Milton Keynes in Buckinghamshire, in their different ways demonstrate that suburbia is admirably flexible and adaptable. It is a blessedly anarchic form.

The accepted wisdom has a long track record of being wrong. Lewis Mumford is half or wholly forgotten by now. But as an urban historian and polemicist, up to his death in 1990, he was regarded as an oracle. What he said, went. He took a dim view of Jane Jacobs muscling in on his territory. In 1962, in a long review of *The Death and Life of Great American Cities* in the *New Yorker*, he loftily derided her 'schoolgirl howlers', her 'inadequate understanding' and her 'amateurish planning proposals'. These were 'no better than applying a home-made poultice for the cure of cancer'. But Jane Jacobs's writing, not Mumford's, became the gospel text that inspired a thousand civic trusts and hundreds of thousands of anti-planning protesters.

The established wisdom about the suburbs – of which Mumford was one bulwark – is just as wrong. We should be grateful for the variety we have inherited. Unity is strength, they say: but diversity is stronger. Tolerance is preferable to intolerance, and libertarianism to dogmatism. The freedoms of suburbia are a fine, humane creation, to be cherished; not an aberration, to be destroyed.

ACKNOWLEDGMENTS

On publication of this essay, my first, heart-felt acknowledgment must be to the Royal Commission for the Exhibition of 1851 (an event that made money, which is still used to fund research). The commission chose me as one of its biennial research fellows in the built environment, with suburbia as the brief. I am extremely grateful for this display of trust. I thank especially Alan Baxter at the commission's fellowship committee. I also thank the Leverhulme Trust for an earlier fellowship, where my brief was to explore aspects of contemporary England.

Successive editors have allowed me space, at different times, to rehearse some of the arguments and observations in these pages. They include the editors of *Prospect* magazine, the *TLS*, the *New Statesman*, the *Evening Standard*, the *Independent* and *Blueprint*. Mary Banham and Jeremy Aynsley invited me to deliver a lecture in the annual Reyner Banham memorial series, held at the Victoria & Albert Museum under the joint auspices of the V&A and the Royal College of Art. I thank all of them.

Many friends and colleagues – from the Young Foundation, the Greater London Group at the London School of Economics and elsewhere – will recognise in these pages clear evidence of innumerable discussions and debates. For me, these were always enjoyable and, I hope they will think, profitable. My deepest thanks to them.

Without Philippa Lewis's assistance – photographs from her Edifice archive, many specially taken, and other picture research – this book would look distinctly wan. I am very grateful for her continued enthusiasm for the project. It has been a pleasure to work with her.

Last but not least, I would like to pay tribute here to the late great Nikolaus Pevsner. His (and his assistants' and successors') *Buildings of England* volumes first inspired me to walk out and about, and to try to understand architecture and cities.

I dedicate this book, with gratitude, to my wife, Sally.

Paul Barker
June 2009

*Englishman's home as castle.
Above left : House converted
into fort, Colchester, Essex.
Above right: Topiary cannon,
Waltham Abbey, Essex. Right:
Highfort Court flats, Kingsbury,
north London (1936), designed
by eccentric architect Ernest
Trobridge to demonstrate
his Swedenborgian belief in
symbolism, hence chimneys
as turrets and entrance as
drawbridge.*

BOOKS

Abrams, Fran, *Below the Breadline: Living Below the Minimum Wage* (Profile 2002)

anonymous, *Suburban Souls: The Erotic Psychology of a Man and a Maid* (?1901; reprinted Wordsworth 1995)

Appleyard, Bryan, *Richard Rogers: A Biography* (Faber & Faber 1986)

Ascher, François, *Métapolis: ou l'avenir des villes* (Paris: Odile Jacob 1995)

Aynsley, Jeremy and Atkinson, Harriet, eds, *The Banham Lectures: Designing the Future* (Oxford: Berg 2009)

Banham, Reyner, *Los Angeles: The Architecture of Four Ecologies* (Allen Lane 1971)

_____, *A Critic Writes* (Berkeley: University of California Press 1996)

Barker, Kate, *Review of Housing Supply: Final Report* (HMSO, 2004)

Barker, Paul, ed., *Arts in Society* (Fontana/ Collins 1977; Five Leaves 2006)

_____, *The Other Britain* (Routledge & Kegan Paul 1982)

_____, *Living As Equals* (Oxford University Press 1996)

Barnes, Julian, *Metroland* (Cape 1980)

Barnett, Anthony and Scruton, Roger, eds, *Town and Country* (Cape 1998)

Bartholomew, James, *Yew and Non-Yew: Gardening for Horticultural Climbers* (Century 1996)

Berger, John, *King: A Street Story* (Bloomsbury 1999)

Betjeman, John, *Collected Poems* (John Murray 1958)

_____, *Coming Home: An Anthology of his Prose 1920–1977* (Methuen 1997)

Bird, John, *Some Luck* (Hamish Hamilton 2002)

Borges, Jorge Luis, *Labyrinths* (Penguin edn 1970)

Brand, Stewart, *How Buildings Learn: What Happens After They're Built* (New York: Viking 1994)

Breheny, Michael and Hall, Peter, eds, *The People – Where Will They Go?* (Town & Country Planning Association 1996)

Bruegmann, Robert, *Sprawl: A Compact History* (University of Chicago Press 2005)

Butler, Tim and Robson, Garry, *London Calling: the Middle Classes and The Re-Making of London* (Oxford: Berg 2003)

Burnett, John, *A Social History of Housing 1815–1970* (Newton Abbot: David & Charles 1978)

Checkland, Sydney, *The Upas Tree: Glasgow 1875–1975* (University of Glasgow Press 1979)

Cannadine, David, *The Decline and Fall of the British Aristocracy* (Yale University Press 1998)

Cohen, Deborah, *Household Gods: The British and their Possessions* (Yale University Press 2006)

Collins, Michael, *The Likes of Us: A Biography of the White Working Class* (Granta 2004)

Conseil Régional d'Ile-de-France, *La Charte de l'Ile-de-France* (Paris: Cahiers de l'Institut d'Aménagement et d'Urbanisme 1991)

Clapson, Mark, *The Invincible Green Suburbs, Brave New Towns: Social Change and Urban Dispersal in Postwar England* (Manchester University Press 1998)

_____, *A Social History of Milton Keynes: Middle England/Edge City* (Frank Cass 2004)

Crouch, David and Ward, Colin, *The Allotment: Its Landscape and Culture* (Faber & Faber 1988; Five Leaves 1997)

Dench, Geoff, Gavron, Kate and Young, Michael, *The New East End* (Profile 2006)

Dennis, Norman, *People and Planning: The Sociology of Housing in Sunderland* (Faber & Faber 1970)

Dunn, Tim, *Bekonscot: Historic Model Village* (Jarrold 2004)

Dyos, H.J., *Victorian Suburb : A Study of the Growth of Camberwell* (Leicester University Press 1961)

Edgerton, David, *The Shock of the Old: Technology and Global History since 1900* (Profile 2006)

Engels, Friedrich, *The Condition of the Working Class in England in 1844* (English edn, including Engels's 'Dedication,' Allen & Unwin 1952)

Frayn, Michael, *Towards the End of the Morning* (Collins 1967)

Gans, H.J., *The Levittowners: Ways of Life and Politics in a New Suburban Community* (Allen Lane 1967)

Garreau, Joel, *Edge City: Life on the New Frontier* (New York: Doubleday 1991)

Ginsborg, Paul, *Italy and its Discontents: Family, Civil Society, State 1980–2001* (Allen Lane 2001)

Girling, Eva and others, *Crime and Social Change in Middle England: Questions of Order in an English Town* (Routledge 2000)

Glazer, Nathan, *From a Cause to a Style: Modernist Architecture's Encounter with the American City* (Princeton University Press 2007)

Gray, Alasdair, *Lanark: A Life in Four Books* (Panther/Granada, 1982)

Greene, Graham, *Complete Short Stories* (Penguin 2005)

Grossmith, George and Weedon, *The Diary of a Nobody* (1892; Penguin Classics, with notes, 1999)

Hall, Peter, *Cities of Tomorrow* (Blackwell 1988, rev. edn 2002)

_____, *Cities in Civilisation* (Weidenfeld and Nicolson 1998)

_____, *The Land Fetish* (Town & Country Planning Association 2005)

Hall, Peter and others, *The Containment of Urban England* (Allen & Unwin 1973)

Hanley, Lynsey, *Estates: An Intimate History* (Granta 2007)

Hardy, Dennis and Ward, Colin, *Arcadia for All: The Legacy of a Makeshift Landscape* (Mansell 1984; Five Leaves 2004)

Hawkins, Jennifer and Hollis, Marianne, eds, *Thirties: British Art and Design Before the War* (Arts Council of Great Britain 1979)

Hayden, Dolores, photographs by Jim Wark, *A Field Guide to Sprawl* (New York: Norton 2004)

Hayes, Dennis and Hudson, Alan, *Basildon: The Mood of the Nation* (Demos 2001)

Hebbert, Michael, *London: More by Fortune than Design* (Wiley 1998)

_____, 'New Urbanism – the Movement in Context,' in *Built Environment* vol 29, No.3 (Alexandrine Press 2003)

Hennessy, Peter, *Never Again: Britain 1945–51* (Cape 1992)

Hobsbawm, Eric, *Interesting Times: A 20th Century Life* (Allen Lane 2002)

Hoskins, W.G., *The Making of the English Landscape* (1955; rev. edn, with notes by Christopher Taylor, Hodder & Stoughton 1998)

Howard, Ebenezer, *To-Morrow: A Peaceful Path to Real Reform* – later re-titled *Garden Cities of To-Morrow* (facsimile of 1st edn, 1898, with commentaries, Routledge 2003)

Hughes, Jonathan and Sadler, Simon, *Non-Plan: Essays on Freedom, Participation and Change in Modern Architecture and Urbanism* (Oxford: Architectural Press 2000)

Hunt, Tristram, *Building Jerusalem: The Rise and Fall of the Victorian City* (Weidenfeld & Nicolson 2005)

Jackson, Alan A., *Semi-Detached London: Suburban Development, Life and Transport, 1900–39* (Allen & Unwin 1973)

Jackson, Kenneth T., *Crabgrass Frontier: The Suburbanisation of the United States* (Oxford University Press 1985)

Jacobs, Jane, *The Death and Life of Great American Cities* (New York: Random House 1961)

Jacobson, Bernard, ed, *Towards a New Landscape* (Bernard Jacobson Gallery 1993)

Jones, G.W. and Donoughue, Bernard, *Herbert Morrison: Portrait of a Politician* (Weidenfeld & Nicolson 1973)

Judd, D.R. and Fainstein, Susan, eds, *The Tourist City* (Yale University Press 1999)

Judt, Tony, *Postwar: A History of Europe since 1945* (Heinemann 2005)

King, Anthony D., *The Bungalow: The Production of a Global Culture* (Routledge & Kegan Paul 1984)

Kureishi, Hanif, *The Buddha of Suburbia* (Faber & Faber 1990)

Kynaston, David, *Austerity Britain, 1945–51* (Bloomsbury 2007)

Laski, Marghanita, *The Victorian Chaise-longue* (Cresset 1953)

Latour, Bruno, *Nous n'avons jamais été modernes* (Paris: La Decouverte 1991; trans. *We Have Never been Modern*, Harvard University Press 1993)

Laver, James, *Taste and Fashion: From the French Revolution to Today* (Harrap 1937)

MacCarthy, Fiona, *William Morris: A Life for Our Time* (Faber & Faber 1994)

Mayor of London, *The London Plan: Spatial Development Strategy for Greater London* (Greater London Authority 2002)

Meacham, Standish, *Regaining Paradise: Englishness and the Early Garden City Movement* (Yale University Press 1999)

Morrison, Kathryn A., *English Shops and Shopping: An Architectural History* (Yale University Press 2003)

Mumford, Lewis, *The City in History: Its Origins, its Transformations and its Prospects* (Secker & Warburg 1961)

_____, *The Urban Prospect* (inc. essay, 'Home remedies for urban cancer,' Secker & Warburg 1968)

Muthesius, Hermann, *The English House* (trans. of *Das Englische Haus*, 1908; Crosby Lockwood Staples 1979)

Muthesius, Stefan, *The English Terraced House* (Yale University Press 1982)

Oliver, Paul, Davis, Ian, and Bentley, Ian, *Dunroamin: The Suburban Semi and its Enemies* (Barrie & Jenkins 1981; Pimlico edn 1994)

Opie, Iona and Peter, *Children's Games in Street and Playground* (Oxford: Clarendon Press 1969)

Owen, Robert, *A New View of Society and Other Writings* (Penguin 1991; first published 1813-49)

Orwell, George, *The Road to Wigan Pier* (Gollancz 1937)

_____, *Coming Up for Air* (Gollancz 1939)

Pahl, R.E., *Urbs in Rure* (LSE and Weidenfeld & Nicolson 1965)

Parkinson, Michael and others, *State of the English Cities* (vols 1 and 2, Office of the Deputy Prime Minister 2006)

Parkinson-Bailey, John J., *Manchester: An Architectural History* (Manchester University Press 2000)

Parr, Martin, *Boring Postcards* (Phaidon 1999)

Pevsner, Nikolaus and others, *Pevsner Architectural Guides* (Penguin 1951–2002, Yale University Press 2002–)

Porter, Roy, *London: A Social History* (Hamish Hamilton 1994)

Power, Anne, *Estates on the Edge: The Social Consequences of Mass Housing in Northern Europe* (Macmillan Press 1997; rev. edn 1999)

Priestley, J.B., *English Journey* (Heinemann 1934)

Rasmussen, Steen Eiler, *London: The Unique City* (abridged rev. edn, Penguin 1960)

Reid, Aileen, *Brentham: A History of the Pioneer Garden Suburb 1901–2001* (Brentham Heritage Society 2000)

Richards, J.M., *The Castles on the Ground* (Architectural Press 1946)

Rogers, Richard and Mark Fisher, *A New London* (Penguin 1992)

Rogers, Richard and Anne Power, *Cities for a Small Country* (Faber, 2000)

Rogers, Richard and others, *Towards an Urban Renaissance: Final Report of the Urban Task Force* (Department of Environment, Transport and Regions 1999)

Saint, Andrew, ed., *Park Hill: What Next?* (Architectural Association 1996)

Saint, Andrew and others, *London Suburbs* (Merrell Holberton/ English Heritage 1999)

Schinkel, Karl Friedrich, *'The English Journey': Journal of a Visit to France and Britain* (new edn and translation, Yale University Press 1993)

Scully, Vincent, *American Architecture and Urbanism* (Thames & Hudson 1969)

Sennett, Richard, *Flesh and the City: The Body and the City in Western Civilisation* (Faber & Faber 1994)

_____, *Respect: The Formation of Character in an Age of Inequality* (Allen Lane 2003)

Silverstone, Roger, ed., *Visions of Suburbia* (Routledge 1997)

Skeggs, Beverley, *Class, Self and Culture* (Routledge 2004)

Smithson, Alison and Peter, *Ordinariness and Light* (Faber & Faber 1970)

_____, *The Charged Void* (2 vols, New York: Monticelli Press 2001)

Sudjic, Deyan, *The 100-Mile City* (Andre Deutsch 1991)

_____, *The Edifice Complex* (Allen Lane 2005)

Sutcliffe, Anthony, *London: An Architectural History* (Yale University Press 2006)

Taylor, Nicholas, *The Village in the City* (Temple Smith/New Society 1973)

Thompson, F.M.L., *The Rise of Respectable Society: A Social History of Victorian Britain 1830–1900* (Fontana/Collins 1988)

_____, ed., *The Rise of Suburbia* (Leicester University Press 1982)

Thompson, E.P., *The Making of the English Working Class* (Gollancz 1963)

Thompson, Flora, *Lark Rise to Candleford: A Trilogy* (Oxford University Press 1945; 3 vols issued separately 1939-43)

Thompson, Michael, *Rubbish Theory: The Creation and Destruction of Value* (Oxford University Press 1979)

Thorns, David, *Suburbia* (MacGibbon & Kee 1972)

Vaughan, Paul, *Something in Linoleum: A Thirties Education* (Sinclair-Stevenson 1994)

Vidal, Gore, *A Thirsty Evil* (Heinemann 1956; edn inc. essay, 'On Pornography,' Four Square 1967)

Watkin, David, *Morality and Architecture* (Oxford University Press 1977)

Ward, Colin, *The Child in the City* (Architectural Press 1978)

_____, *Social Policy: An Anarchist Response* (LSE 1997)

_____, *Cotters and Squatters: Housing's Hidden History* (Five Leaves 2002)

Watson, Winifred, *Miss Pettigrew Lives for a Day* (Methuen 1938; Persephone 2000)

Webber, Melvin, ed., *Explorations into Urban Structure* (Philadelphia: University of Pennsylvania Press 1964)

Whitehead, Christine and Scanlon, Kathleen, eds, *Social Housing in Europe* (LSE 1997)

Wilkinson, Adam, *Pathfinder* (SAVE Britain's Heritage 2006)

Williams, Tim and others, *Quality First: The Commission on the Design of Affordable Housing in the Thames Gateway* (Housing Corpn 2007)

Williams-Ellis, Clough, *England and the Octopus* (Bles 1928)

_____, (ed.) *Britain and the Beast* (Dent 1937)

Willmott, Peter, *The Evolution of a Community: A Study of Dagenham after 40 Years* (Routledge & Kegan Paul 1963)

Wodehouse, P.J., *Big Money* (Herbert Jenkins 1931)

Wolfe, Tom, *From Bauhaus to Our House* (Cape 1982)

Young, Michael and Willmott, Peter, *Family and Kinship in East London* (Routledge & Kegan Paul 1957; rev. edn Penguin 1962; new edn 2007)

INDEX

Page numbers in *italic* refer to captions